FOOD WEIRD-O-PEDIA

The Ultimate Book of Surprising, Strange, and Incredibly Bizarre Facts about Food and Drink

ALEX PALMER

Skyhorse Publishing

Skyhorse Publishing books may be purchased in bulk at special discounts for sales promotion, corporate gifts, fund-raising, or educational purposes. Special editions can also be created to specifications. For details, contact the Special Sales Department, Skyhorse Publishing, 307 West 36th Street, 11th Floor, New York, NY 10018 or info@skyhorsepublishing.com.

Skyhorse® and Skyhorse Publishing® are registered trademarks of Skyhorse Publishing, Inc.®, a Delaware corporation.

Visit our website at www.skyhorsepublishing.com.

10 9 8 7 6 5 4 3 2 1

Library of Congress Cataloging-in-Publication Data available on file.

Cover design by Kai Texel

Print ISBN: 978-1-5107-6374-6
Ebook ISBN: 978-1-5107-6573-3

Printed in China

contents

INTRODUCTION

Food is fundamental. We eat it every day and in a huge variety of ways. Whether straight from a tree or out of the ground, whipped up in our kitchen at home or purchased in a drive-through, we all have many connections with food, some deeply personal. The smell of a particular dish may trigger a memory of a family dinner or an unforgettable meal we enjoyed while traveling to a new place. Our preferences for a specific spice or way of preparing a classic dish can lead to heated debate with friends and strangers alike. A certain meal or drink can provide comfort during a difficult time and even remind us of who we are and what's important to us.

Every one of us has a complex relationship to the food we eat, each as unique as we are. But there is also a lot that can surprise us about what we put in our body—unexpected facts about staple fruits and veggies, strange backstories to our favorite sweets, and ways of preparing a familiar dish that are downright weird. These odd aspects of the food we eat are what *Food Weird-o-Pedia* is all about. This book offers up hundreds of off-kilter bits of info about food that will make you say "no way!" and maybe even rethink what you know about foods you've been eating your whole life.

Organized in general sections covering major food categories such as fruits, vegetables, meat, and snacks, each chapter in this book offers an alphabetical "encyclopedia" of strange facts that will give you plenty to chew over, whether reading from cover to cover or just flipping to a random page during a lunch break. We hope you enjoy *Food Weird-o-Pedia* and that it provides plenty of fodder to impress friends and family over your next meal—whatever it is you're eating.

CHAPTER 1

FRESH FRUIT

Sweet slices of info about your favorite fruits

APPLES

Apples are about 25 percent air. This is why a freshly picked apple makes that satisfying cracking sound when you take a bite out of it—and why they float so well in bobbing-for-apples barrels.

The apples sold at your produce aisle could have been picked as long as a year ago. Farmers use a technology called "controlled atmosphere storage" that regulates not just the temperature but levels of humidity, nitrogen, and carbon dioxide in which the fruit is stored. The process puts the fruit into a kind of hibernation that slows its ripening.

> Apples tend to store best in high humidity, so a simple and surprisingly effective way to preserve the fruits is to wrap them in a damp paper towel and put them in the fridge or put them in a plastic bag, making sure to poke holes in the bag to release the ethylene gas they give off as they ripen.

Apple seeds can be poisonous. Those innocent-looking pips contain the compound amygdalin, a molecule that when broken down produces the poisonous gas hydrogen cyanide. Fortunately, each seed contains a very small amount of amygdalin, meaning you would have to eat the seeds of dozens of apples before things started getting risky. A number of fruit pits actually contain a higher concentration of the compound (apricot pits, for example, contain almost five times more per gram). But the likelihood you'll mistakenly eat an apricot pit, let alone the many required to seriously endanger your life, is even more remote.

The heaviest apple ever recorded weighed four pounds, one ounce (1.849 kilograms), grown by a farmer on his apple farm in Hirosaki City, Japan, and picked on October 4, 2005. The largest bowl of applesauce was produced in Riddes, Switzerland, on October 27, 2018, as part of a charity drive. It weighed almost 860 pounds (390 kilograms).

APRICOTS

Apricots originated in China more than four thousand years ago. From there, they spread to Persia and the Mediterranean before Spanish missionaries brought them to North America. Its Arabic name of *amardine* translates to "moon of the faith."

One of Apple Computers' early competitors was Apricot Computers, a British producer of PCs that produced the first commercial shipment of an all-in-one system with a 3.5-inch floppy drive *before* that more famous fruit-named computing company. It was eventually acquired, then shut down, by Mitsubishi Electric Corporation.

AVOCADOS

Avocados were once known as "alligator pears," a moniker coined by naturalist Sir Hans Sloane in his 1696 catalog of plants. Early in its cultivation in the United States, Florida stuck with the more colorful name even as California adopted "avocado," due to the fruit's arrival from Mexico, where it was known as *aguacate*. Eventually the United States Department of Agriculture approved "avocado" as the official name.

Despite bananas' reputation as one of the food world's most potassium-packed fruits, avocados actually contain higher levels of the mineral. One avocado contains about as much potassium as two to three of the yellow fruit.

The Spanish conquistadors of Central and South America not only enjoyed eating avocados, they used their pits to produce ink to compose documents, many of which survive today (the documents, that is, not the conquistadors).

BANANAS

Bananas help other fruits ripen. Many fruits give off the hydrocarbon gas ethylene as they near readiness to eat, which accelerates not only their own further ripening but that of any fruits nearby. Bananas produce ethylene at a particularly high rate, so if you put a browning banana in the same bowl as your apples and avocados, it will speed up the ripening of all its fellow fruits.

> A bunch of bananas is known as a "hand" and individual bananas are referred to as "fingers."

Banana peels have a number of medicinal properties. The polysaccharides on the inside of the peel help to alleviate the itch of bug bites. The peel's astringent salicylic acid helps reduce plaque while its citric acid serves as a gentle bleaching agent to help with teeth whitening. Enzymes on the inside of the peel actually encourage splinters to move toward the skin's surface, so applying a hunk of banana peel to a place where a sliver has lodged itself can prove more effective, and less painful than a pair of tweezers.

BLACKBERRIES

Life Savers candy attempted to swap the orange-flavored candy with blackberry in 2003—after the five flavors of orange, lemon, lime, cherry, and pineapple had remained unchanged for nearly seven decades. The change did not go over well and blackberry was soon swapped back out.

While the fruit of blackberries is delicious, other parts of the plant have been used for medicinal purposes for centuries. For example, in the English county of Somerset, those suffering from bronchitis were advised to carry a blackberry shoot to nibble on when they started coughing, while in Scotland, the leaves were reputed to relieve burns, swelling, and even toothaches.

BLUEBERRIES

Blueberry was one of several food-scented Magic Scent crayons that Crayola discontinued in 1995 after parents complained that they smelled so enticing that their children would be tempted to eat them (according to a spokesperson for the crayon company, they had received fewer than ten reports of children actually eating the crayons, and no injuries).

Blueberries are often confused with huckleberries. Both belong to the same family and share a similar appearance, with some dark-colored blueberries and blue huckleberries, but there is one clear way to distinguish the two: blueberries contain many fine seeds, while huckleberries contain ten larger seeds (also known as "nutlets"). So next time you're chomping on some berries and trying to figure out just what they are, look for the nutlets.

There are five major varieties of blueberries in the United States: rabbiteye, southern highbush, northern highbush, lowbush, and half-high.

CHERRIES

Cherries may have killed Zachary Taylor, the twelfth president of the United States. On the hot day of July 4, 1850, after leaving a fundraiser at the Washington Monument, the sixty-five-year-old leader "ate heartily of cherries and wild berries, which he washed down with copious draughts of iced milk and water" to refresh himself, as his son told Taylor's doctor later. He soon was suffering from severe cramps and on the night of July 9, he died in the White House of "cholera morbus." Though speculation of his cause of death persists, historians agree that it was likely something he ate, making cherries a top suspect.

Japan's Yamanashi prefecture is home to the oldest cherry blossom tree in the world. Called Jindai-zakura, or "the cherry blossom from the age of the gods," it is estimated to be roughly two thousand years old.

COCONUTS

Cherries may have killed one president, but coconuts saved the life of another. During World War II, John F. Kennedy and his crewmates were stranded on a small island for two days with nothing but coconuts to provide them nourishment. Eventually they made it to a larger, neighboring island and were able to find inhabitants, to whom Kennedy passed a hunk of coconut, with the message "NAURO ISL . . . COMMANDER . . . NATIVE KNOWS POS'IT . . . HE CAN PILOT . . . 11 ALIVE . . . NEED SMALL BOAT . . . KENNEDY." The message was received, Kennedy's crew was rescued, and, upon becoming president, he used the carved coconut as a paperweight on his Oval Office desk.

While coconuts can save lives, they can also be deadly. No, not because those falling from trees can cause deaths (it's an oft-repeated falsehood that "falling coconuts kill 150 people each year") but because palmitic acid derived from coconut oil is one of the key ingredients to napalm. When combined with naphthenic acid (the "na" to palmitic acid's "palm") and mixed with gasoline, the incendiary mixture proved destructive, deadly, and inexpensive, and killed hundreds of thousands throughout the Vietnam War. So next time you sip your coconut water, remember that this fruit has a dark side.

FIGS

Figs are pollinated by tiny fig wasps. It works like this: A tiny, pregnant wasp enters a small opening at the end of the fig, often losing its wings and antennae in the process. It deposits pollen that it's carrying from the flower in which it was born, then lays its larva . . . and dies inside the fig. Those eggs hatch and the baby wasps then make their way out of the fig, bringing the pollen with them to help spread the fruit's genetic material elsewhere. The carcass of the queen wasp then is broken down into protein, which unsuspecting fig fans consume with every fruit they pop into their mouths. So next time you take a bite of a fig, know that there's a chance you're munching on a dead wasp carcass.

GRAPEFRUIT

This citrus fruit tastes nothing like a grape, so where does its name come from? When seen growing on a tree, the fruits grow in clusters that can appear like a bunch of oversized, yellow grapes. When unripe, the grapefruit's green hue particularly enhances its resemblance to giant green grapes. Just don't try popping one into your mouth all at once.

When the grapefruit was first introduced to the West after its discovery in Barbados, Welsh naturalist Griffith Hughes called this hefty yellow citrus "forbidden fruit." While there is debate about what he considered so forbidden about it, researchers have more recently discovered that grapefruit can have some unpleasant reactions with certain types of medications. While grapefruit's high levels of vitamin C and potassium make it generally very healthy, the juice has been found to let more of certain drugs (such as those meant to lower cholesterol or treat high blood pressure) enter a person's blood, increasing the medications' side effects. This could result in liver and muscle damage or even kidney failure. The United States Food and Drug Administration has taken to putting warnings on certain drugs, urging patients to avoid drinking grapefruit juice or eating grapefruits. In other words, at least for some people taking certain medications, grapefruit is indeed "forbidden."

 ## GRAPES

In the United States, grapes are often the least-interesting ingredient in a fruit salad, but in Japan, they are highly prized—at least, specific varieties of grape. The very sweet Ruby Roman grape, about the size of a Ping-Pong ball, were developed in 2008 and have become highly valued for their flavor and texture. How prized? In 2019, a bunch of twenty-four grapes sold for 1.2 million yen (about US $11,000).

The people of Spain and parts of Latin America practice a New Year's Eve tradition in which they eat twelve green grapes at the stroke of midnight. Known as *uvas dee la suerte*, the tradition is believed to have begun in the Alicante region of Spain, as grape farmers sought to get rid of their surplus harvests. But it has developed into a full-blown superstition, with each grape believed to represent a month of the year and those who fail to finish their grapes within the clock's chimes will be bound for misfortune over the next twelve months.

In New Zealand, "kiwi" usually refers only to the flightless national bird that serves as a nickname for the people of New Zealand and is rarely used to describe the green fruit. So be careful when ordering kiwi in your fruit salad.

KIWI

This fuzzy fruit is most often associated with New Zealand, which exports more than $1 billion of the product annually. But it had previously been associated with a very different part of the world. Better known in the early twentieth century as "Chinese gooseberry," named for the north-central and eastern Chinese region to which it is native, it was rebranded in the 1960s by New Zealand exporters. After briefly dubbing the fruit a "melonette," the name "kiwi" finally stuck.

LEMON

Lemon season never ends. While the peak harvest tends to run from late winter to early summer, lemon trees continuously produce, and the sour fruits can be picked any month of the year.

Lemon juice can indicate whether you are an introvert or extrovert. Researchers have found that introverts tend to have higher levels of arousal in the Reticular Activating System (RAS) area of their brains, which responds to stimuli such as food and social interaction. This naturally higher level of RAS activation in introverts leads them to feel sufficiently stimulated in smaller, quieter groups (while extroverts' lower levels of arousal leads them to seek greater stimulation, interacting with more people) but also causes an increased salivary response to some foods, including lemons. Scientists have found that a few drops of lemon juice causes an introvert to produce a much greater amount of saliva than an extrovert, whose lower level of RAS activity requires a higher level of stimulation to be activated. So if you're not sure whether you're an introvert or extrovert, suck on a lemon and see what happens.

Sweet lemons were once a thing. In the late 1920s, a variety of lemons the size of grapefruits and as sweet as oranges were developed by growers in Puerto Rico. They gave off a sweet scent that led locals to pop a couple of them into their linen closets for weeks of fresh scents. But they proved more popular for smelling than eating and soon became hard to find in the average produce aisle.

LIMES

Ever notice that while most lemons have seeds, most limes do not? That's because most limes sold in the United States are Persian limes, a hybrid of true limes and citron that is produced without fertilization. Instead, farmers typically use grafting techniques to more or less clone one tree onto a new one, allowing for the production of more limes.

ORANGES

Not all oranges are orange. The color is caused by a breakdown in chlorophyll in the citrus fruit's skin, so in subtropical regions where it does not get cold enough for this to occur, the chlorophyll is preserved and the fruit remains yellow or green even once it's ripe. But they still call the fruit an "orange."

Why is the fruit called "orange"? Not because of its color, it turns out. The word derives from the Arabic *naranj* (believed to have meant "fragrant"), which became *narange* in English in the fourteenth century. The "n" was eventually dropped and the fruit ended up with the familiar, unrhyme-able name we use today. The word wasn't used to refer to a color for another two hundred years.

PAPAYAS

The black seeds of papaya fruit can be dried, ground, and sprinkled onto dishes as an exotic alternative to black pepper.

PEACHES

You're familiar with the typical round peach, but there's another variety that is flat, less fuzzy, and juicier than a typical peach and known by the appetizing name of "donut peaches." Also known as "UFO peaches," "galaxy peaches," "sweet bagels," and "sauzee swirls," these saucer-shaped fruits become trendy every few years. While they might seem genetically designed for Instagram, they are naturally occurring.

> The only difference between a peach and a nectarine is that a peach has fuzz and a nectarine does not.

Georgia may be famous for its peaches, but it produces fewer of them than the states of California, South Carolina, and New Jersey.

PEARS

These days, pears are far from the most popular fruits. However, there was a time when people went crazy for the things. When early European colonists first introduced pears to North America in the nineteenth century, a "pear mania" went through New England's upper class. From around 1820 to 1870, it became fashionable for gentlemen who could source pear seeds to serve up the exotic fruits to visitors to their homes as a sort of male bonding activity, along with golf and cigars. Once pears began to be produced in California in large quantities, the allure dropped off and pear mania subsided.

"Pear cider" is actually something of a misnomer. Cider is an alcoholic beverage made from fermented apples—and *only* apples, with a few rare exceptions. An alcoholic beverage made from fermented pears is known as "perry." The drink was popular in England for centuries but fell out of favor during the second half of the twentieth century. That turned around in the 1990s when the drink was rebranded "pear cider."

PINEAPPLES

Pineapple works as a natural meat tenderizer. The fruit is packed with the enzyme bromelain, which breaks down protein chains, making it an ideal marinade for meats, turning it soft and sweet at the same time. But for the same reason, pineapple does not work for jams or jellies, since the enzyme also breaks down gelatin. The bromelain is so strong, that pineapple processors have to wear protective gloves, otherwise over time the enzyme eats away at the skin on their face and hands, leaving dry skin and small sores.

The world's largest maze, according to the *Guinness Book of World Records*, is the Pineapple Garden Maze at the Dole Plantation on

Oahu, Hawaii. Covering three acres, with two and a half miles of paths, and consisting of more than fourteen thousand plants, it includes eight stations that create a game for visitors, with a pineapple-shaped garden in the center. It takes about an hour for the average visitor to make it to the middle, but the current record holder completed it in just seven minutes.

RASPBERRIES

Raspberries are not actual berries—and neither are strawberries. In botanical terms, a berry is a fruit that develops from one flower that has one ovary. This disqualifies both raspberries and strawberries, which have flowers with more than one ovary. However, blueberries and cranberries are true berries—as are bananas, eggplants, tomatoes, and avocados (seriously).

Why do we call that vulgar sound we make by putting our tongue between our lips and blowing out a "raspberry"? You can thank the Brits, whose Cockney rhyming slang used "raspberry tart" to rhyme with . . . well, you can probably guess. It eventually got shortened to just "raspberry."

The galaxy tastes like raspberry. Astronomers analyzing a giant dust cloud in the heart of the Milky Way found that it contained ethyl formate, the substance that gives raspberries their flavor. Of course, even if you manage to procure some space dust, it might not be wise to try it yourself; the researchers also found the poisonous chemical propyl cyanide in the same cloud.

STRAWBERRIES

The typical red garden strawberry most of us think of when we hear "strawberry" is actually just one of a number of the fruits that are out there. Strawberry enthusiasts can also seek out the pineberry, which has a pale color accented with red specks, making it look like a regular strawberry that's had the color drain from its face, and which has a sweet, pineapple-like flavor. The reddish-brown creamy strawberry grows in Finland and is appreciated for its sweet flavor. The Himalayan strawberry has a light pink color (and an apparently less-than-pleasant taste).

It is sometimes said that strawberries are the only fruit that wears its seeds on the outside or that the average strawberry holds about two hundred seeds. However, those seedlike bits on the fruit's skin aren't actually seeds, they are small fruits themselves, known as "achene," each of which contains its *own* tiny seed. To reproduce, strawberries don't generally rely on these seeds, but on parts known as "runners" that grow out from the main strawberry plant, until they find new ground in which to plant themselves and grow.

> Seventeenth-century writer Dr. William Butler said of strawberries: "Doubtless God could have made a better berry, but doubtless God never did."

The small Belgian town of Wépion is home to the Musée de la Fraise, or "Strawberry Museum." Visitors can learn about the history of the fruit and its impact on the local economy, shop for jams, candies, and strawberry beer, and take a tour of the thirty-five-acre fruit garden.

WATERMELONS

Watermelon rinds are not only edible but also packed with health benefits. Although we tend to throw out the green part of the melon after snacking on its refreshing, pink pulp, the rind has been found to be rich in fiber, reduce blood pressure, and may even improve one's sexual performance (at least, one peer-reviewed study found the citrulline amino acid it contains benefited men with moderate erectile dysfunction). No wonder it's common to eat the rind in other parts of the world like China and the Middle East. Imagine eating a cucumber—a cousin to the watermelon—by slicing it into wedges and eating around the dark green skin, and you've got a sense of how other cultures view American reluctance to eat the watermelon skin.

Watermelon is both a fruit and a vegetable—depending on who you ask. While it falls under the botanical definition of a fruit, since it is the ripened ovary of a seed plant which itself includes seeds, many others consider it a vegetable. This includes the people of Oklahoma, who named the watermelon the state's official vegetable in 2007.

CHAPTER 2

CRISP AND CURIOUS

Nourishing facts about vegetables

ARTICHOKES

An artichoke is actually a flower that has not yet matured. If left to grow on the tip of the artichoke plant, they blossom into bright purple flowers (and taste a lot worse).

In 2010, a Miami doctor sued a Houston restaurant after he'd ordered the grilled-artichoke special . . . and ate the entire thing. Not realizing that a person should stick with eating just the soft heart of the artichoke or the "meat" that can be scraped off the individual leaves, he'd also managed to consume every one of the tough, pointy leaves. Severe abdominal pain led him to go to the hospital and he eventually sued the restaurant for "bodily injury, resulting pain and suffering, disability, disfigurement, mental anguish, loss of capacity for the enjoyment of life, medical and nursing care and treatment, and aggravation of pre-existing conditions." Did I mention he was a doctor?

When she was twenty-two years old, Marilyn Monroe (then going by the name Norma Jean) was crowned Artichoke Queen by judges in Castroville, California. While the title might make you think she won an artichoke-eating contest or earned the distinction in some other artichoke-related way, in fact, the farming community about fifteen miles northeast of Monterey and home to an annual Artichoke Festival had little criteria for the honor beyond that the recipient be appealing and available. In 2006, it awarded William Hung, famed at the time for his distinctive audition on *American Idol*, with the honor of Artichoke King.

ASPARAGUS

Asparagus makes pee smell weird—but only for a lucky few. Benjamin Franklin described a "disagreeable odour" after eating a few stems of the stuff while Marcel Proust blamed the vegetable for "transforming my humble chamber into a bower of aromatic perfume," but they are actually in the minority of those whose urine is aromatically affected by asparagus. Scientists believe the smell is caused by a substance called asparagusic acid that gains the scent as it's being processed through the body. However, studies have found that only a fraction of subjects—ranging from about

20 percent to about 40 percent—actually notice the smell. So if your pee smells weird after eating asparagus, consider yourself, along with Franklin and Proust, to be part of the exclusive stinky-pee club.

White asparagus is basically just asparagus that needs a tan. While this variety of the vegetable is extremely popular in a number of European countries, thanks to its slightly sweeter flavor and hint of bitterness, the pale color is often incorrectly assumed to be related to its genetic makeup. In fact, the color just comes from the fact that white asparagus is grown underground. Farmers cover the vegetable in a mound of dirt as it grows, protecting it from any contact with sunlight and preventing it from producing chlorophyll. As the tips of the spears finally begin to pop above the soil's surface, they must be picked by hand and placed immediately in a dark container to keep them free from exposure.

BEETS

Humans originally skipped the deep-red root and ate the large, leafy beet greens, which have a similar texture and taste as chard. When they did use the root, it was usually as medicine for ailments including headaches, toothaches, and skin problems, rather than food.

Beets were served as a celebratory offering during the height of the Cold War. In 1975, during the Apollo-Soyuz Test Project,

Soviet cosmonauts welcomed the American astronauts aboard Apollo 18 during a US–USSR test project with tubes of space food filled with borscht. To add some fun to the exchange, the Soviets pasted vodka labels over the tubes of beetroot soup. The Americans toasted with the tubes and slurped up the contents anyway.

BROCCOLI

This cruciferous veggie actually contains more vitamin C than oranges, with 132 mg of the vitamin per serving—almost twice the 69.7 mg of vitamin C found in an orange.

Why don't we see canned broccoli in stores, next to the canned carrots, peas, and beets? It has to do with appearance. Preparing vegetables for canning requires them to be heated first to kill off any bacteria, then again under steam pressure. While many vegetables maintain their color and texture during this process, it turns broccoli florets into mush and leaves them with a grayish-green color that looks anything but appetizing. So, if fresh broccoli isn't an option, frozen florets are the way to go.

The English used to call broccoli "Italian asparagus."

"Broccoli" is the sixth-most commonly misspelled word in the English language. According to a separate report from Google, it is also the *most* misspelled word in Google searches in the state of Minnesota.

It might have been a coincidence, but the "Oldest Cat Ever," according to the Guinness World Records, ate broccoli as part of her standard diet, along with bacon, eggs, turkey, and coffee—plus an eyedropper of red wine every two days. The cat lived to the age of thirty-eight.

BRUSSELS SPROUTS

To raise money for cancer research, in 2015, adventurer Stuart Kettell rolled a Brussels sprout to the top of Mount Snowdon in Wales. It took him three days to reach the peak of the 3,560-foot (1,085-meter) mountain, since he opted to add drama by rolling the sprout with his nose.

As you may have assumed, this plant gets its name from the Belgium city of Brussels, where it was widely cultivated possibly as far back as the thirteenth century. Yet descriptions as late as 1796 suggest that they were originally appreciated more for the leaves at the top of the stalk than the miniature cabbage heads growing along it.

CARROTS

Carrots are actually healthier for you when they are cooked. Studies have found that the vegetable's level of beta-carotene and antioxidants are higher when consumed cooked rather than raw.

Carrots may be good for you, but be careful not to overdo it or you might start looking like one. Because of their high levels of beta-carotene, eating a lot of carrots can lead to a condition known as carotenemia, which has the distinctive symptom of turning a person's skin a slight orangey color. While carotenemia is both relatively harmless and rare (you'd have to eat about ten carrots a day for a few weeks for it to develop), it can also be caused by consuming large amounts of other beta-carotene-rich foods such as pumpkin, cantaloupe, and apricots. It tends to first appear in areas of the body where skin is a bit thicker—palms, knees, elbows—so if you've been eating a lot of orange foods lately, keep an eye on these spots before you wake up looking like a carrot.

When the root part of carrots were being eaten in the Arab world around the tenth century, they were purple or dark red. The earliest signs of orange carrots don't show up until the seventeenth century, in Dutch paintings depicting the vegetable in this hue (purple carrots are still grown in Afghanistan).

CAULIFLOWER

If white cauliflower seems a bit too pallid for your taste, agricultural scientists have developed varieties of the vegetable in purple, green, and orange (or "cheddar") colors. Like that more familiar orange vegetable, orange cauliflower contains high levels of carotene, which converts into vitamin A in the body—about 300 times the levels found in white cauliflower.

CELERY

During the 1960s, Jell-O was available in celery flavor. It was part of the brand's "for salads" line that also included "mixed vegetables," "seasoned tomato," and "Italian salad."

> Celery might not seem like the sexiest of vegetables, but in fact, it is a natural aphrodisiac. It is loaded with the male hormone androsterone, which, if eaten, releases a scent that boosts the arousal in females. So on your next date, skip the wine and order a Bloody Mary.

CORN

During certain times of the season, you can actually hear corn grow. Crop experts have claimed that on particularly quiet nights, as the cell walls of the stalk expand, it creates an audible cracking sound. Part of this is because the crop grows fast—an inch or more in a matter of hours during the peak time of the season.

There is (almost) always an even number of kernels on an ear of corn. This is because of the corn's "spikelets" which are produced in pairs—one fertile, one sterile—leading to an even number of rows. Occasionally, something can go wrong during development, leading a row to fail to fully mature and for what appears to be an odd number of rows. In the rare cases where these are found, the odd cob is considered good luck—akin to a four-leaf clover.

Sweet corn is the type we typically eat—purchasing it frozen, canned, or fresh on the cob. But this makes up only 1 percent of all corn produced in the United States. The vast majority is field corn, which is much less tasty but much more useful. This is the stuff that goes into corn cereal, corn syrup, livestock feed, ethanol, and all sorts of other products. It's also known as "dent corn" because of the dimple that appears on each kernel as the corn dries.

> Corn is produced on every continent in the world—except Antarctica.

CUCUMBER

Cats are afraid of cucumbers. There is no shortage of online videos showing unsuspecting cats stumbling upon cucumbers and freaking out—jumping a foot in the air or running in the opposite direction as if their lives depended on it. Turns out, they think their lives do depend on it. Animal behaviorists theorize that the cat mistakes the produce for a snake or some other predator. While it might seem like a hilarious prank, those same behaviorists caution that no one should try this at home—stressing out your pets can cause long-term emotional damage.

The most cucumbers sliced from a person's mouth with a sword in one minute is 57. The skilled swordsman who accomplished this feat is Jamaica, New York, local Ashrita Furman, who broke his own record from two years prior of slicing 46 cucumbers (Furman actually holds more than 200 Guinness World Records).

EGGPLANT

Known as "aubergine" in England and elsewhere, Americans dubbed this veggie "eggplant" due to a specific white-skinned variety that really does resemble an egg. But by the mid-nineteenth century, it was the term used for all the aubergine varieties, including the more familiar, bulbous purple type that looks nothing like an egg.

> But long before that, eggplant was known as "the mad apple" in Europe due to the belief that it caused insanity in those who consumed it.

GARLIC

A number of myths identify garlic as evil. In India, the vegetable was believed to be desired by demons; a Buddhist myth holds that garlic arose from the blood of a demonic spirit killed by the god Vishnu; while Islamic tradition holds that it originated from Satan's left foot. These associations helped feed the opposite belief: that garlic can also repel evil spirits. Ancient Italians wore cloves as a defense against "the evil eye," and garlic has been used in exorcisms in India and England. And, of course, the pungent vegetable is known to be a defense against vampires.

However, a certain kind of real-world vampire loves garlic. In a study published in *The Journal of the Norwegian Medical Association* in 1994, a pair of researchers found that while it took leeches an average of 44.9 seconds to attach themselves to a clean hand, it took them just 14.9 seconds to attach themselves to a hand smeared with garlic. The researchers' tongue-in-cheek conclusion: "This study indicates that garlic possibly attracts vampires. Therefore, to avoid a Balkan-like development in Norway, restrictions on the use of garlic should be considered."

KALE

While we now are more likely to associate kale with celebrity diets and overpriced salads, it once had a much less upmarket reputation. The vegetable has been grown in Europe for more than two thousand years and was as likely to be fed to livestock as humans. For that reason, it earned the nickname "peasant cabbage." While it was widespread in Germany, the Netherlands, and Scotland (whose residents coined the term "kail" and called their small gardens "kailyards"), it was seen as a vegetable of last resort. As its impressive health benefits became better understood, tastemakers in the United States were soon touting its nutritional value and its reputation rapidly rose. By the early 2010s it had become a celebrated superfood.

> Before the kale craze took off, one of the biggest purchasers of the leafy green in the United States was Pizza Hut, which used kale to decorate its hundreds of salad bars across the country.

As healthy as it may be, eating kale raw can be tough on the digestive system—causing bloating and all sorts of unpleasantness. Studies have also found that raw kale does not have the cholesterol-lowering benefits that are released when kale is cooked. On the other hand, researchers have found that the cancer-fighting benefits of kale are more likely to be delivered in raw form. So . . . maybe have a little of both?

 ## MUSHROOMS

The world's largest living organism is a mushroom. Specifically, it's a single honey fungus of the species *Armillaria ostoyae* in the Malheur National Forest Oregon's Blue Mountains. Nicknamed the "humongous fungus," it spreads across more than 2,200 acres and is estimated to be about 2,400 years old. While its size is impressive, its growth is not exactly welcome—it's a parasite that attacks the roots of coniferous trees and slowly kills them. Talk about throwing your weight around!

The *Laetiporus* genus of mushrooms is commonly known as "chicken of the woods." Why? Because it tastes like fried chicken. It's a popular ingredient in stir-fries, pasta sauces, and omelets, and serves as a convenient plant-based replacement for meat.

The *Gyromitra esculenta*, better known as the "brain mushroom," due to its resemblance to a human brain, not only looks kind of gross, but is deadly if eaten raw. Nonetheless, it is considered a delicacy in Scandinavia, Eastern Europe, and elsewhere. In 2015, Swedish chef Paul Svensson created a furor when he prepared a dish using the deadly mushroom on a cooking show. Experts criticized him for encouraging home cooks to whip up a potentially deadly dish (though there were no reports of any viewers dying after trying it at home).

ONIONS

Images of onions decorate Egyptian tombs dating back to almost 3000 BCE. They were presented as religious offerings, set on altars, and even used to prepare the dead for burial. Onions have also been found flowering from the chest cavities of mummies.

Want to put a stop to all those tears that start when chopping an onion? One of the most effective ways to prevent the tear-inducing gas (known officially as Syn-propanethial-S-oxide) released while cutting the vegetable from reaching your eyes is to do your chopping under running water. Or you can wear goggles, if dignity is not important to you.

POTATOES

Why do we call potatoes "spuds"? The word first appeared in English in the fifteenth century as a generic term for tools for digging (likely derived from the Dutch word *spyd* for "short dagger"). Over time, the word came to refer not only to an instrument used for retrieving tubers from the ground ("spade"), but for the tubers themselves ("spud").

PUMPKINS

The canned "pumpkin" that goes into pumpkin pie is mostly butternut squash. The USDA is lenient about distinguishing between the two, so cans of pumpkin puree can claim to be "100 percent pumpkin" even when it's made of one or more types of winter squash, such as Hubbard, Boston Marrow, Golden Delicious, and, most commonly, butternut.

Pumpkin pie may be a staple of every Thanksgiving table today, but there's little chance it was something the Pilgrims actually ate at the first Thanksgiving—or the twentieth. It wasn't until the early eighteenth century that the orange-crusted custard began to make appearances as part of this celebration.

Almost all of the United States' pumpkins are produced in Illinois, with the state generating more pumpkins than the three next-highest producers combined. According to the University of Illinois, 80 percent of all the pumpkins produced commercially in the United States are sourced from within a ninety-mile radius of the city of Peoria. The state dominates in part because of soil and weather conditions that are conducive to the squash, but mostly because the state got a head start on the pumpkin-processing business, setting up factories as early as the 1920s, and maintaining its hold on the industry ever since.

RADISHES

Radishes are a key part of Christmas celebrations in Oaxaca, Mexico. December 23 is known as Night of the Radishes, when those in the area create elaborate sculptures portraying the nativity, local lore, and famous figures using, you guessed it, radishes. Carving oversized tubers specially cultivated in the region (which can grow to five pounds or more), the artists compete with one another in several categories, with the grand-prize winner taking home about US $1,000 and bragging rights that last for years.

> Radishes were highly esteemed by the ancient Greeks, frequently mentioned by writers including Dioscorides and Pliny the Elder. Small gold replicas of radishes were even placed in temples as symbols of devotion to the god Apollo (replicas of beets and turnips served a similar purpose, but were typically made from baser, less valuable metals).

RHUBARB

Rhubarb is delicious, especially when baked up with lots of sugar and strawberries into a pie. But while the reddish-pink stalks might taste good, the leaves of this vegetable definitely do not. This part of the rhubarb contains high levels of oxalic acid, which, if ingested, binds to calcium ions, removing them from the blood and causing illness and potentially death. It may also form insoluble calcium oxalate, which can lead to kidney stones. Thankfully, it requires a *lot* of rhubarb leaves—like, several pounds—to kill you.

January 23 is National Rhubarb Pie Day, but National Strawberry-Rhubarb Pie Day doesn't take place until June 9. Be sure you don't mix up these dates or you might show up with the wrong pie—very embarrassing!

 ## SALAD

Caesar salad is not named after Roman leader Julius Caesar, but the salad's inventor, Italian restaurateur and hotelier Caesar Cardini, who came up with the idea of combining romaine lettuce, Parmesan cheese, and raw egg yolk at his Tijuana restaurant.

The Cobb salad was created by accident. As the story goes, in 1937, Robert H. Cobb (aka Bob Cobb), owner of L.A. eatery The Brown Derby, was feeling hungry and threw together the ingredients he happened to have lying around the kitchen: romaine, watercress, tomatoes, chicken, hard-boiled egg, cheese, and some leftover bacon—topped with some of the Derby's signature French dressing. Cobb's friend, Sid Grauman—of Grauman's Chinese Theatre fame and husband of silver-screen goddess Gloria Swanson—was there that night, and the concoction caught his eye. He ordered it for lunch the next day and soon it was one of the restaurant's most popular dishes.

The longest salad bar measured 688 feet, 1.56 inches (209.74 meters) long, created by Jensen Jewelers in Hudsonville, Michigan, as part of the city's first Salad Bowlbash, celebrating the local agriculture on July 27, 2013. The salad ingredients themselves—a mix of lettuce, carrot, onion, radish, cabbage, zucchini, celery, cucumber, and peppers (to count as a "salad" according to Guinness, it had to include at least four vegetables)—weighed more than two thousand pounds.

The phrase "salad days"—referring to a person's time of youth and inexperience—was coined by William Shakespeare in *Antony and Cleopatra*. Cleopatra, describing her regrets about her relations with Julius Caesar in her younger days, says ". . . My salad days, / When I was green in judgment, cold in blood/To say as I said then!"

SAUERKRAUT

Many are familiar with the story of how Scottish naval surgeon James Lind, working to identify a way to overcome the scurvy that was decimating British sailors during the eighteenth century, struck on citrus fruits as the most effective cure. While the fruit would eventually become a standard supply on every naval ship and earn the British their "limey" nickname, at first it had some competition. A number of naval leaders, notably Captain James Cook himself, swore by the healing power of sauerkraut. Cook ensured barrels of the stuff was put aboard his ships (on its voyage to the

South Pacific in 1768, the HM Bark *Endeavor* carried 7,860 pounds of the fermented cabbage). He was not too far off—sauerkraut is actually rich in vitamin C, which was the key to fighting scurvy—but it only has about one-fifth the vitamin C of a lemon or lime.

 ## SPINACH

Spinach can neutralize explosives. Research by the US Department of Energy found that nitroeductase enzymes, found naturally in spinach, have a reactivity effect that degrades explosives and provides a safer way to dispose of explosive material than burning, detonating, or burying it—though it will likely be some time before bomb squads include bunches of spinach in their equipment packs.

Speaking of strange uses for spinach, biomedical engineers found that the vegetable's leaf structure worked well as scaffolding in which beating human heart cells could be grown. The researchers cleared out the plant cells in the spinach leaves, using a special detergent solution, and replaced them with human heart cells. This turned the leaves into a natural (and less expensive) alternative to the synthetic apparatuses more typically used for growing layers of heart muscle that is used to treat heart-attack victims and others receiving heart-cell transplants. The research is still in its early stages, but certainly shows that spinach is even more heart-healthy than we realized.

TOMATOES

Tomatoes are fruits—but in the United States, they are legally vegetables. Botanists define fruits as the seed-bearing part of a plant that develops from its flower, while all other parts of the plant (leaves, roots, stems, and tubers) are the vegetables. So, technically, cucumbers, peppers, and squash also are all fruits. Weirdly, thanks to an 1893 US Supreme Court case settling an issue between a food importer who wanted to label his tomatoes as fruits (which had a lower import tax) and a tax collector who asserted that they were vegetables. The court ruled that the tomato is most commonly known as a vegetable and should be taxed as such. Although botanists would disagree, the ruling has held to this day.

For two centuries, Europeans believed tomatoes were poisonous and avoided eating them, even dubbing them "poison apples." This wasn't just based on suspicion of their red color: a number of people who ate them did get sick or even died, particularly the wealthy. The reason for this was that the high acidity of tomatoes, when placed on the pewter dishes that were popular among the well-to-do, would cause the fruits to leach lead from the plate. Once ingested, it would cause lead poisoning, leading to the illness.

YAMS

Nigeria's adaptation of *Sesame Street* includes Zobi, a version of Cookie Monster who drives a cab and, instead of cookies, is partial to yams. Since the tuber is more accessible to local kids, and healthier than cookies, the show's producers opted to make the switch. As he says in one episode: "What is so exciting about yams? Everything!"

CHAPTER 3

FUN WITH FLOUR

Surprising facts about breads, cereal, grains, and baked goods

BAGELS

The NCAA once banned cream cheese on bagels for students receiving full scholarships. As part of their scholarships, these students were permitted three meals a day and provided with fruits, nuts, and bagels throughout the day as snacks, but once cream cheese (or butter, jam, or any spread) was added to the bagel, it was considered an additional "meal," and they'd be charged for it.

Bagels were once considered an ideal "push present" for pregnant women. The earliest mention of bagels was in a 1610 regulation issued by the Jewish council of Krakow, Poland, "which stated that bagels would be given as a gift to any woman in childbirth," according to Leo Rosten, author of *Joys of Yiddish*. Other interpretations of the regulations read it as saying that bagels are a gift that a midwife can provide to her attendants to celebrate a successful delivery.

The bagel's shape has always been central to its identity. The word "bagel" is derived from the German word *bougel*, which means "ring" or "bracelet." The shape also proved convenient for bagel makers as it allowed them to more easily stack on a wooden dowel or to string them together (which was popular among wholesale bakeries in the 1970s). But the reason the hole is there in the first place? To help them bake faster, with more surface area for the amount of dough—and more of that caramel-brown crust.

BAGUETTES

The French consume 320 baguettes every second, according to Observatoire du Pain (France's "Bread Observatory"—yes, that's a thing.) That's an average of half a baguette per person per day, or ten billion of the crusty loaves annually.

Every year, Paris hosts Le Grand Prix de la Baguette, in which hundreds of bakers each prepare two of their best baguettes for a fourteen-member panel to judge. It might seem like it would be hard to tell one of these baked goods from another, but the judges must assess each based on five criteria: baking, appearance, smell, taste, and "crumb." The winner does not receive a cash prize, but earns a gold seal they place in their bakery window, and are also granted the honor of providing a loaf to the French president.

BREAD ROLL

Practically as long as restaurants have existed, they have offered complimentary bread rolls or other baked items before meals. However, this practice has had its detractors over the years. In 1912, a number of New York City's high and hotel restaurants began charging ten cents for premeal bread, as a means to offset costs and reduce waste. A century later, the debate continues to rage, with *ABC News* reporting "Free Bread at Restaurants Hitting Endangered Status" as several restaurants across the country began charging. In another article on the topic, in *Restaurant Hospitality*, a restaurateur offered a compromise: "Now the servers ask after the salads if guests would like bread with their meal. We have saved a ton in wasted dough."

CEREAL

When they were first introduced in 1941, Cheerios were originally named CheeriOats. The name was shortened to Cheerios four years later.

Tony the Tiger may be the familiar mascot of Kellogg's Frosted Flakes, but he was only selected after a competition with three other potential mascots. However, when the American public were able to choose, they were just not as into Katy the Kangaroo, Elmo the Elephant, or Newt the Gnu (it probably didn't help that most people didn't know what the heck a gnu was).

The first breakfast cereal had to be soaked in milk overnight. Created from graham flour dough that was dried and broken, the cereal, known as "granula" was introduced in 1863 and would later inspire the pebble-hard cereal Grape-Nuts.

In the 1930s, an early version of Wheat Chex was introduced as Shredded Ralston. The weird name came from the fact that it was targeted to followers of Ralstonism, a racist self-help movement that urged strict guidelines around diet and exercise, to improve one's magnetism and better influence the thoughts of others (eventually bringing about a new, superior race). A dedicated Ralstonite would practice exercises such as walking on the balls of their feet and moving in graceful arcs and would start their day with a hearty bowl of whole wheat Shredded Ralston.

CIABATTA

The word ciabatta translates to "slipper" in Italian, due to the shape of the loaf.

Ciabatta might seem like an old-world staple, but it was actually invented just a few decades ago. It was in the early 1980s that Italian miller Arnaldo Cavallari, frustrated by the volume of French baguettes being imported into his native Rome, determined that Italy should have its own local alternative. Experimenting with a number of different doughs, and eventually adding a lot of water to the recipe, he produced the soft loaf. It quickly caught on in his native country, and within a few years, was being distributed throughout the United States and theUK.

ENGLISH MUFFINS

Today, we only really know of "the muffin man" as a character in a nursery rhyme. However, in Victorian England, he was a very familiar—and to some, an obnoxious—figure. The muffin man would stroll the town streets at teatime, delivering English muffins (which they just called "muffins") door to door, ringing a bell as he went along. This probably sounds kind of charming to modern readers, but in the 1840s, the daily ringing irritated the English people enough that the muffin man's bell ringing was prohibited by an act of Parliament. The muffin men promptly ignored it and continued on their noisy way.

A "baker's dozen" was not always thirteen. The practice of adding an extra loaf of bread or muffin to an order is believed to have begun by bakers looking to avoid being penalized for shorting customers (which was strictly enforced in twelfth-century England). As recently as 1864, John Hotten's *Slang Dictionary* defined a baker's dozen as "thirteen or fourteen; the surplus number, called the inbread, being thrown in for fear of incurring the penalty for short weight."

GRAHAM CRACKERS

Graham crackers were created to tamp down a person's sex drive. Reverend Sylvester Graham was a tireless advocate for dietary reform, urging Americans to embrace vegetarianism, temperance, and eat whole-grain bread, not only to be healthier but as a means to keep one's sexual urges in check. His teachings gained many influential followers and led to the development of graham flour, made from whole grain, ground more coarsely and not sifted the way whole-wheat flour is processed, as well as graham crackers.

Though these caught on as a snack, once Nabisco Biscuit Company began to produce them for a mass audience, sugar and spices were soon added to the recipe. They proved an enduring hit, even if they might not be as healthy for one's waistline or libidinal discipline as the good reverend would have liked.

OATS

Just 4 to 5 percent of the world's oat harvest is consumed by humans—the rest is eaten by livestock. The biggest human use is, of course, cereal—oatmeal, Honey Bunches of Oats, Cracklin' Oat Bran, and so on. The biggest non-cereal use? Oatmeal cookies, followed by . . . meatloaf.

In Samuel Johnson's 1755 dictionary, he cheekily defined oats as "a grain, which in England is generally given to horses, but in Scotland appears to support the people." Scottish lord, and friend of Johnson, Patrick Murray, replied, "That's why England has such good horses, and Scotland has such fine men!"

Forget chocolate chips; oatmeal cookies were by far the most popular homemade cookie in the early twentieth century, with many cookbooks featuring several recipes for the sweet treat. The wide availability and affordability of oats made them an ideal ingredient for those looking to whip up a cheap and delicious dessert. (Chocolate chips wouldn't even become widely available until the 1940s.)

PIZZA

Pizza didn't really become popular in the United States until after the Second World War. While there had been a handful of pizza places in a few major cities dating back to the early twentieth century (most famously Lombardi's, opened in New York City's Little Italy neighborhood in 1905), it was not until after World War II that it became a national favorite. Historians attribute this to returning American GIs, who had gotten a taste for the savory dish while in Naples and sought it out upon their return— with a few particularly American twists.

Pizza wasn't originally something you would eat for lunch. In one of the earliest accounts of the now globally popular dish, a writer for London's *Morning Post* described his travels in Naples in 1860 and that the Neapolitan pizza "is only made and eaten between sunset and two or three in the morning." While that practice has certainly changed, one thing that hasn't: Everyone loved pizza. As he wrote, "in the pizza shops rich and poor harmoniously congregate; they are the only places where the members of the Neapolitan aristocracy—far haughtier than those in any other part of Italy—may be seen masticating their favourite delicacy side by side with their coachmen, and valets, and barbers."

Hawaiian pizza was invented in Canada. Sam Panopoulos, owner of an Ontario pizzeria, came up with the idea of tossing pineapple on a pie in 1962.

Chicago's Pizzeria Uno, where deep-dish pizza is reputed to have been invented, began as a Mexican restaurant. Liquor-company executive Ike Sewell and tavernkeeper Ric Riccardo went into business on a place that would serve up Mexican classics, prepared by one of Riccardo's bartenders—until they actually tried his food, got violently ill, and realized they needed a Plan B. Riccardo headed off for vacation to Italy and returned with the inspiration to bring pizza to the Windy City, but in a style that would work as a meal rather than an appetizer, and Chicago-style pizza was born.

> Technically, the bottom of the pizza is referred to as the "crust" while the outer edge is properly referred to as the "cornicione" (pronounced "cor-nee-cho-nay"), as in cornice or molding.

PRETZELS

That shopping-mall staple Auntie Anne's sells some unusual pretzel flavors overseas. One of its most popular varieties in Singapore is the seaweed-flavored pretzel, in Saudi Arabia its stores serve up date-flavored pretzels, while in the UK, they go all-in for banana flavored.

Pretzels may have helped save the day in Old World Vienna. Legend has it that in 1510, Turks from the Ottoman Empire set about invading the Austrian city with a surprise subterranean attack. They began digging tunnels under the city walls, aiming to enter Vienna in the middle of the night when everyone was asleep— well, almost everyone. The city's bakers (renowned for their pretzel-making) were up long before the sun was to rise and detected the digging, alerting the military and thwarting the attack. The bakers were awarded an official coat of arms by the city council for their help.

RICE

The Philippines is home to the International Rice Gene Bank. Maintained by the International Rice Research Institute, the bank holds more than 132,000 species of rice and its wild relatives, accessible to researchers throughout the world. Scientists and organizations can submit seed requests and, if approved, are sent samples for their research, breeding, or training efforts. As far as we could tell, there have been no attempted robberies on this bank so far.

Is tossing rice at weddings a form of animal cruelty? In 1985, Connecticut state legislators attempted to ban celebratory rice slinging out of fear it would cause "injury and death of birds as a result of ingesting raw rice thrown at weddings." There was a widespread belief at the time that the uncooked rice expanded in the birds' stomachs and caused them to have violent deaths, as one of the bill's advocates explained. Once reporters actually asked a few bird experts if this was a risk, they were quickly set straight that the whole thing was a birdbrained myth. Cornell ornithologist Steven Sibley explained: "Rice must be boiled before it will expand. Furthermore, all the food that birds swallow is ground up by powerful muscles and grit in their gizzards. Many birds love rice, as any frustrated rice farmer will tell you."

SANDWICH BREAD

Wonder Bread didn't used to be sliced. According to documents from the US Patent & Trademark Office, the product was introduced on May 1, 1921, as an unsliced loaf. It would be nine years before "Wonder-Cut" bread hit grocery shelves. Within a couple years, it was selling both regular slices and a thin-sliced variety, especially popular for those making dainty finger sandwiches for tea. In the 1960s, the brand even rolled out a round-slice variety—a better fit for bologna or burgers.

Sliced bread started hitting grocery store shelves in 1928 and was advertised as "the greatest forward step in the baking industry since bread was wrapped." That slogan helped inspire the popular expression "the greatest thing since sliced bread."

> The US Department of Agriculture actually has an official policy of what can be defined as a "sandwich": "Product must contain at least 35 percent cooked meat and no more than 50 percent bread." Of course, plenty of sandwiches can be made without meat and still be considered a sandwich—at least by Merriam-Webster's definition: "two or more slices of bread or a split roll having a filling in between."

In the 1920s and 1930s, the United States saw the rise of a panic about bread. Led by a diet guru who dressed in leopard skin, this mass fear, known as *amylophobia*, held that white bread not only lacked nutritional value, but actually caused illnesses including diabetes, tuberculosis, kidney disease, and more. As bread makers began adding vitamins to their recipes and tastemakers pushed back against the hysteria, the fear subsided, and love for bread came back strong.

In 1943, the United States banned sliced bread. Meant as a way to create savings during wartime by cutting down on production and packaging costs (sliced bread required heavier wrapping than unsliced), it turned out "the savings are not as much as we had expected," the head of the US Food Administration ended up determining at the time. So after less than two months, sliced bread was back.

SOURDOUGH

A two-thousand-year-old loaf of sourdough bread was uncovered in what was once the ancient town of Herculaneum, next to Mount Vesuvius. Ancient Roman bakeries were in the practice of stamping loaves with the date and location it was produced, so, thanks to the carbonization caused by the eruption of the nearby volcano, archaeologists were able to determine it was baked on August 24 in the year 79 CE. "Toast" is an understatement.

TORTILLAS

Tortillas have been outselling hot dog and hamburger buns in the United States since 2010 and consistently sell more than white bread. The CEO of the Tortilla Industry Association (yes, that's a thing) has pointed not only to the changing demographics in the country, but the growing variety of tortillas on offer—whole wheat, low carb, spinach, sundried tomato, and even beetroot.

For sales-tax purposes, New York State defines burritos to be "sandwiches." But in 2006, a court in the state of Massachusetts ruled that "under this definition, this court finds that the term 'sandwich' is not commonly understood to include burritos, tacos, and quesadillas, which are typically made with a single tortilla and stuffed with a choice filling of meat, rice, and beans." So the definition of "burrito" truly depends on where you live.

Tortillas used to be sold in cans. It was an innovation of restaurateur and canner George Ashley of El Paso, Texas, who provided them to members of the US military during World War II. That continued to be a popular packaging for the product under General Mills' Old El Paso brand, until the 1990s.

WHEAT

Most of the bread marketed in the United States as "wheat" is actually white bread that has been dyed brown with caramel food coloring. If you're looking to pick up a healthier loaf, don't just trust the label that calls it "7 grain" or "multi-grain"; double check that the first ingredient begins with "whole" rather than "enriched."

There are thousands of varieties of wheat, but just six classes: hard red winter, hard red spring, soft red winter, hard white, soft white, and durum.

All but eight states in the U.S. grow wheat, with Kansas and North Dakota alternating as the biggest producer, depending on the year. It's quite adaptable, grown both at sea level and in places such as Tibet that are more than four thousand feet above sea level.

CHAPTER 4

CARNIVOROUS CRAVINGS

Things you didn't know about meat and seafood

BACON

Bacon was the first meal eaten on the moon. Well, technically it was bacon cubes, specially stored to allow for space travel, which Neil Armstrong and Edwin "Buzz" Aldrin enjoyed along with peaches, a pineapple grapefruit drink, coffee, and sugar-cookie cubes (cubes were the go-to format for space food).

Bacon was used to help make explosives. During World War II, Americans were encouraged to donate the fat rendered from their cooking (particularly bacon) so the Army could convert the fats to glycerin, which could then be applied to more destructive purposes. The US government went so far as to create the American Fat Salvage Committee to guide this effort and produce videos such as one featuring Disney's Minnie Mouse and Pluto explaining the process and why the fat was so important.

Bacon and eggs may seem like the perfect breakfast combo, but it was not always that way. Up until the early nineteenth century, a typical American breakfast consisted of a cup of coffee, a roll, and maybe a cup of juice—nothing fancy. But in the 1920s, Edward L. Bernays, later celebrated as the "father of public relations," was trying to figure out how to increase Americans' consumption of bacon (the main product of his client at the time, Beech-Nut Packing Company). He launched a campaign that incorporated thousands of physicians advocating the benefits of a healthy breakfast, including bacon and eggs. The dubious health advice earned plenty of headlines, sales of bacon spiked, and "bacon and eggs" became a match made in breakfast heaven.

BARBECUE

The world's longest barbecue lasted eighty hours, wrapping up on April 27, 2014. Conducted entirely by pitmaster Jan Greeff in the city of Columbus, Georgia, in partnership with grill brand Char-Broil, it included the cooking of 1,000 hot dogs, 200 pieces of corn, 104 pieces of chicken, 558 burgers and 526 boereworse (a sausage from Greeff's native South Africa) over the three days.

The event raised more than ten thousand dollars for the Juvenile Diabetes Research Foundation.

> The record for world's longest barbecue (in terms of length, not time) was achieved the same month as Greeff's accomplishment by a team in the Philippines municipality of Bayambang, in the province of Pangasinan. Created by connecting 8,000 grills at the Malangsi Fishtival, the mega-grill measured 8,000 meters (20,246 feet) and required 6,000 bags of charcoal to cook up the day's fish.

Barbecue ribs go back to prehistoric times. In 2009, researchers uncovered a four-foot cooking pit in the Czech Republic that they estimated dates back to 29000 BCE. Complete with cooking utensils such as spatulas and saws, it also contained the sizable ribs of a gigantic mammoth. The archaeologists were unable to determine if the ribs had been slathered in sauce or a dry rub.

BEEF

A bite from a common tick can trigger an allergy to red meat. Scientists have recently found that a bite from a Lone Star tick can transmit a sugar molecule called alpha-gal into a person's body, causing an immune system reaction that can later result in sometimes severe allergic reactions to red meat that can cause symptoms including hives, shortness of breath, and stomach pains.

Five countries in the world contain more cows than people: Uruguay, New Zealand, Argentina, Australia, and Brazil. Uruguay has more than three-and-a-half times as many cows as humans.

CHICKEN

Fried chicken was invented in Scotland. While baking or broiling was the most common way of preparing poultry in eighteenth- and nineteenth-century kitchens, in Scotland it became popular to panfry the meat in fat. As Scots immigrated to the United States, it is believed they brought this cooking style with them, where it flourished, particularly in the South.

In Japan, Christmas is celebrated with a bucket of Kentucky Fried Chicken. Considering the relatively few Christians in the country, the holiday was not widely celebrated, but in 1970, Takeshi Okawara, the manager of the first KFC in Japan, overheard a couple foreigners discussing how they missed their Christmas turkey. He jokingly suggested KFC as an alternatively festive fowl—then realized that was actually a pretty great idea. He was soon promoting a holiday Party Barrel at his store, and as more KFCs popped up on the island nation in subsequent years, KFC's corporate marketing department launched a national Kentucky for Christmas campaign. It proved a hit, and families still gather together on the holidays over a bucket of chicken and Colonel Sanders in a Santa suit becomes a common sight. These special Christmas dinner packages constitute about a third of the company's annual sales in Japan.

Why do so many meats "taste like chicken"? One theory is that a chicken's chest, from where much of its meat is taken, contains white "fast-twitch fibers" that allow it to move quickly when a threat is detected—fibers that are found in other animals, along with low concentrations of the protein myoglobin, which tend to be found in much higher concentrations in animals that require more endurance.

There are more chickens on the planet than any other bird—quite a few more. There are about twenty-three billion chickens on

Earth at any given time, which is at least ten times more than the second-most-numerous bird. Combined, the mass of chickens is more than *all* other birds on Earth.

 # EGGS

The most egg yolks ever found in a single egg is nine.

Alfred Hitchcock, director of such hair-raising thrillers as *Psycho* and *The Birds*, was terrified of . . . eggs. "I'm frightened of eggs, worse than frightened, they revolt me," he once said. "That white round thing without any holes . . . have you ever seen anything more revolting than an egg yolk breaking and spilling its yellow liquid? Blood is jolly, red. But egg yolk is yellow, revolting. I've never tasted it."

Don't be impressed by eggs that advertise themselves as "hormone free." The FDA has banned the use of hormones in poultry production going back to the 1950s, so a package of eggs promoting its lack of hormones is like a box of cereal promising that it is free of chunks of scrap metal—it should really go without saying.

The thickness of an egg's shell is related to the age of the chicken that laid it—the older the chicken, the thinner the egg. *And* you can tell the age of an egg by dropping it in a glass of water. As they age, air moves into the porous shell, creating air pockets and causing the egg to be more buoyant. The more it floats, the more air; and the more air, the older it likely is.

> Not only do chickens have earlobes, but the color of their lobes allows you to predict the color of their eggs. The fowl have no outer ear, but they do have visible lobes, which range from white to nearly black—those with white lobes lay white eggs, and those with darker-colored lobes lay darker brown eggs. The Araucana breed of chickens even sport pale green or blue lobes—and produce the eggs to match.

GOAT

The myotonic breed of goat is popular for meat production in the Southern US, but it is most famous for its habit of falling over when startled. Nicknamed the Tennessee Fainting, Stiff-Legged or Nervous goat, this quirky animal has a genetic condition known as myotonia congenita, which causes the muscles to tense when it becomes excited. Despite its "fainting" moniker, it doesn't actually lose consciousness, just the ability to move its legs.

 ## HAM

The difference between a "city ham" and a "country ham" has nothing to do with from where the preserved pork comes. Country ham is salt-cured and usually smoked with hickory or red oak and stored at room temperature, while city ham is brine-cured and has to be kept refrigerated (and is the kind you're most likely to put on a sandwich). Likewise, Canadian bacon is not necessarily from Canada.

However, there are plenty of more geographically specific types of hams, as well. These include:

- **Smithfield ham**—Aged country ham cured in a particular way in the city of Smithfield, Virginia, for a minimum of six months. Virginia law used to require that Smithfield pigs be fed with peanuts, but that stipulation was dropped in 1966.

- **Westphalian ham**—Made from pigs fed with acorns from Germany's Westphalia Forest, then smoked over a mix of beechwood and juniper woods.
- **Éisleker ham**—A product of the Oesling region in northern Luxembourg, it comes from the hind legs of pigs and is brine-cured for a couple weeks before being smoked in oak chips (though they used to be hung in chimneys and smoked that way).
- **Njeguški pršut** — A specialty of the Montenegro city of Njeguši, this ham is dry-cured with sea salt, smoked over beechwood, and cooled with mountain breeze before it's ready to eat—a process that takes about a year.

 ## HAMBURGERS

In 2003, animal-rights organization People for the Ethical Treatment of Animals offered the city of Hamburg, New York, $15,000 to change its name to Veggieburg. The PETA spokesperson explained that, "The town's name conjures up visions of unhealthy patties of ground-up dead cows." The city's officials declined the offer.

In 2010, a waitress at a McDonald's restaurant based in Holland was fired for selling a coworker a hamburger and then allowing them to add a slice of cheese separately without charging, rather than charging the full price for a cheeseburger. She took them to court for wrongful termination and was awarded $5,900. As the court stated in its written judgement: "The dismissal was too severe a measure. It is just a slice of cheese."

People have put strange things on their hamburgers, but a pop-up food stand that appeared in London in 2013 may take the bun for grossest burger toppings. Launched by pest control company Rentokil to celebrate its 85th anniversary, the burger included salted weaver ants, barbecued crickets, and chocolate-covered worms. Oh, and the burger itself was made of sweet-chili pigeon. I guess that if you buy a burger from an exterminator, you might expect it to be not particularly appetizing.

HOT DOGS

Hot dogs were originally known as "red hots." The classic origin story is that German immigrant Charles Feltman struck on the idea of putting a traditional frankfurter into a bun while selling pies on a pushcart in New York's popular Coney Island beach destination. He dubbed it "Coney Island red hot" and the convenience of being able to grab the snack and hit the beach made it a hit with the beachgoers.

Feltman is not the only person to lay claim to the title of "inventor of the hot dog." Anton Feuchtwanger, another German immigrant, who sold sausages on the streets of St. Louis, Missouri, came upon the idea (well, his wife made the suggestion, as the story goes) of offering customers a bun so they would not burn their fingers on the dog.

Despite their names, "Michigan-style" dogs (in which the dog is topped with a thick, tomato-based sauce) is popular in upstate New York, while "coney dogs" (topped with meat chili, chopped onions and mustard and named after New York's Coney Island) is biggest in Detroit. Meanwhile, a "Texas hot dog" topped with chili or hot sauce, is mainly popular in Pennsylvania.

The world's longest hot dog was made to celebrate Paraguay's two hundredth anniversary as a country. The country may not be known as a hot-dog hot spot, but at the 2011 Expoferia in Asuncion, Paraguay, the 203.8 meter (668 foot, 7.62 inch) tube steak was produced by local butcher Ochsi. The bun had to be baked on a conveyor belt to keep it all intact—a key requirement to earn the record. While Sara Lee Corp. created a 608-meter (1,996-foot) hot dog in commemoration of the 1996 Summer Olympics in Atlanta, Georgia, the bun was not continuous, so it was denied the distinction.

One of the favorite offerings in Taiwan's night markets are Da Chang Bao Xiao Chang—also known as "Big sausage wrap small sausage." It's just as it sounds: a hot dog weiner, with a larger sausage serving as its bun. Definitely the "meat-lover's" favorite.

LAMB

"Mutton" comes from the Latin word *multo*, referring to any male sheep. Since males were most likely to be sent to slaughter than milk-producing females, the word became the generic term for sheep meat. In a number of Caribbean islands—and Asian countries including Bangladesh, Pakistan, and India—the word "mutton" is used to describe both goat and sheep meat.

The world's top consumer of sheep meat, on average, is Sudan, where 23 pounds (10.5 kilograms) of mutton is consumed per capita. This is followed by Kazakhstan (18 pounds/8.1 kilograms), Australia (16 pounds/7.4 kilograms), and Algeria (16 pounds/7.1 kilograms).

LOBSTER

Lobster shells have been used to make biodegradable golf balls. Engineered by researchers at the University of Maine, these eco-friendly balls cost just about nineteen cents for the materials. They were designed for use on cruise ships, allowing passengers to whack them into the ocean without worrying about creating long-term pollution.

> Ben & Bill's Chocolate Emporium in Bar Harbor, Maine, is famous for its Lobster Ice Cream. With a butter-flavored ice cream base, the creamery mixes in cooked meat from a local lobster pound for a strangely sweet concoction.

Lobsters urinate out of their faces. When they need to relieve themselves, the urine is excreted from glands set near the antennae (they do not "pee out of their eyes" as is sometimes claimed). The peeing actually accomplishes a complex range of communication, whether the crustaceans are fighting or mating. One more reason to be glad you eat the lobster tail rather than the head.

Speaking of lobsters' weird anatomy, they also have teeth in their stomachs, their brains are in their throat and they hear using their legs while tasting with their feet.

Lobster did not used to be viewed as the delicacy we consider it today. So abundant and disrespected was the shellfish, that a law was passed in one Massachusetts town that forbade serving it more than three times to indentured servants. Native Americans used lobsters to fertilize their crops and as bait for fishing.

 ## OYSTERS

Oysters are always in season. A culinary rule of thumb once held that raw oysters should only be consumed in months that contain the letter "r," skipping them during the summer months when unrefrigerated oysters would be more likely to spoil. However, advances in food safety, and refrigeration, have made this truism an anachronism today. So, even in the height of summer, feel free to slurp up those bivalves.

Jonathan Swift once said, "He was a bold man that first ate an oyster."

The most expensive oyster in the world may be Coffin Bay King oysters. Sourced from a farm in a peninsula along the South Australia coastline, these shellfish have a particularly strong flavor and firmly tender texture that has earned it the moniker "the oyster steak of the ocean." They are also huge, with some weighing as much as two pounds and costing about $75 apiece.

> While there are hundreds of varieties of oysters, there are just five species: Pacific Oysters (or Japanese Oyster), Kumamoto Oysters, European Flat Oysters, Atlantic Oysters, and Olympia Oysters.

PORK

According to the United Nations Food and Agriculture Organization, pork is the most widely eaten meat in the world, accounting for 36 percent of the world's animal-protein intake. This is followed by poultry at 33 percent, beef at 24 percent, and goats/sheep at just 5 percent.

Prehistoric pigs once roamed the earth. Technically named entelodonts, these prehistoric creatures stood up to seven feet tall and could weigh as much as two thousand pounds, with a set of dangerously sharp teeth and powerful jaw muscles. The largest animal to live in North America since the dinosaurs, it thrived for about twenty million years before going extinct during the Miocene era, about sixteen million years ago. Its nastiness has earned it the nickname of "hell pig"—it no doubt would have produced some tough pork chops.

If someone were to literally "sweat like a pig" they would not be sweating at all. Pigs don't have sweat glands, and roll around in the mud in order to keep cool. But another cliché, "to eat like a pig" is a bit more accurate. Pigs are indeed omnivorous, largely indiscriminate eaters who will pretty much eat whatever is put in front of them.

The pork tenderloin sandwich is a staple culinary offering in the state of Iowa, but there is local debate about whether it's best enjoyed breaded or grilled. In 2004, while visiting the Top Notch Tavern in the city of Brookston, Governor Mitch Daniels asked the waitress which was better there, but she refused to make a choice. Daniels recounts that, "They agreed to bring me half breaded, half grilled. It later went on the menu as 'Daniels' Dilemma.'"

SALAMI

The largest diamond heist in history was undone by a salami sandwich. A team led by Italian mastermind Leonardo Notarbartolo used infrared light to fool the sensors of Belgium's Antwerp World Diamond Centre, and disabled heat detectors with hair spray, then used a slab of aluminum to redirect the magnetic field that kept the vault door locked. The clever moves allowed them to escape with $100 million worth of diamonds. But the jewelry thieves blew their cover by dumping their garbage on the side of the road where it caught the eye of a local. Authorities found envelopes from the Antwerp Diamond Centre, CCTV tapes from the vault, and a half-eaten salami sandwich. DNA evidence from the sandwich connected it back to Notarbartolo, who eventually confessed.

SPAM

Few people actually know what "Spam" stands for. While most assume it is short for "spiced ham" (and that's probably correct), Hormel Foods' official position is that the name "is known by only a small circle of former Hormel Foods executives." Ken Daigneau, the brother of a company executive, is one of those in the know—he came up with the name, winning $100 in prize money.

Spam, which became widespread during World War II as part of soldiers' rations, earned a few unkind nicknames among the GIs: "ham that didn't pass its physical," "meatloaf without basic training," and "the reason war is hell."

> Spam is incredibly popular in the state of Hawaii, where an annual Waikiki Spam Jam is held during the last week of April, with entertainment, booths selling Spam-themed merchandise, and, of course, plenty of salty Spam dishes.

SUSHI

Uni is not sea urchin—it's the genitals of sea urchins. The creamy, tongue-shaped delicacy is often one of the priciest items on a sushi menu and advertised as "sea urchin," but in fact, it is the gonad, or genital gland of the sea creatures. It contains milt and roe during the urchins' spawning season and is packed with nutrients, which helps give the uni its distinct flavor and texture.

Almost all wasabi sold in the United States is not wasabi. About 99 percent of the stuff is actually a mix of horseradish, mustard, and green dye. The real stuff comes from the wasabi plant, sold by the stem and served freshly grated, which is quite a bit more expensive than the powdered horseradish concoction served in most restaurants.

One of Japan's oldest forms of sushi is *funazushi*, which can take as long as five years to prepare. A Japanese carp known as *nigorobuna*, which is only found in Lake Biwa, in Japan's Shiga Prefecture, is packed in salt and left to ferment in a wooden barrel for a year. It is then dug out, mixed with rice, and packed back up for fermenting another two to four years before it's ready to eat. Its taste has been described as tangy, fishy, and even ammonia-like. However, it's an in-demand delicacy for anyone who makes it to the area.

 ## TUNA

Tuna's bland taste was what helped it to catch on with consumers. "Nobody ate tuna before 1900," according to Andrew Smith, author of *American Tuna: The Rise and Fall of an Improbable Fish*, who says, "It was considered a trash fish." But as developments in canning and fishing technology (and overfishing of sardines, at the time the most popular canned fish) allowed for more to be caught and processed and more pleasingly presented, it began to gain popularity, driven by marketing that promoted how much it tasted like chicken and could easily blend into a casserole or salad without a distractingly strong fish flavor. It turned out that boring was a brilliant marketing strategy and within a couple decades tuna would be America's most popular fish.

CHAPTER 5

BETWEEN-MEAL TIDBITS

Curious facts about snacks

 ## ALMONDS

Almonds have long been considered an aphrodisiac. In the biblical tale of Samson and Delilah, the shaggy strongman uses flowering almond branches to try and attract the attention of his love interest. In Greek mythology, the gods turn grieving princess Phyllis into the first almond tree, which has fueled its esteem as a symbol of romance ever since. More recently, French novelist Alexandre Dumas viewed almond soup as an effective means of arousal. And sugar-covered almonds have long been a traditional wedding favor. Talk about almond joy . . .

> While the shells of almonds are inedible to humans, that doesn't mean they go to waste. These hulls are often used as bedding for livestock or fed to cows. More recently, researchers have been looking into how the material can be turned into compostable dinnerware or used in the brewing of beer and hard cider.

For something a little different, snack fans can try green almonds. These lightly sweet treats are essentially baby almonds, plucked from the tree while the shell is still a fuzzy, soft green and has yet to harden. The whole thing can be eaten, providing a slightly crunchy texture (though softer than a ripened almond) and a tart, nutty flavor. But because timing is so sensitive in their development, they're only available for a few weeks each spring, so get 'em while they're soft!

CHEETOS

There are some unusual flavors of Cheetos around the world. Japan is home to Pepsi- and strawberry-flavored Cheetos (as well as Hello Kitty–flavored Cheetos, whatever those taste like). Hungary has peanut Cheetos and India has masala-ball Cheetos.

The Cheetos spokesanimal used to be not a cool cheetah, but a mouse.

CRACKERS

In October 2015, a cracker sold at auction for £15,000 (more than $18,000). The Spillers and Bakers biscuit made of flour and water didn't fetch that price because it was especially delicious. At more than one hundred years old, it would probably be inedible. The reason it was such a hot seller was that it came from a survival kit in one of the *Titanic*'s lifeboats. Passenger James Fenwick, one of the lucky few who survived the ship's sinking in 1912, held on to the biscuit for decades until his descendants opted to sell it. Its sale earned it the title "the world's most valuable biscuit" as it dwarfed the previous highest seller: A £3,000 cracker from Antarctic explorer Ernest Shackleton's 1907 expedition in which he made it to within 112 miles of the South Pole—by far the closest any person had made it at the time.

> The small holes in crackers such as saltines are put there by a spiked cylinder called a "docker" that punctures the dough in order to prevent air bubbles from forming and ruining the cracker's appearance.

The phrase "Polly want a cracker?" was popularized as an advertising slogan for Nabisco's saltine crackers. The phrase had been in use since at least 1849 (in a satirical cartoon where a man says it as he winds up to strike a parrot) and also appeared in Robert Louis Stevenson's *Treasure Island* in 1883, but it was as an advertising slogan that it first became widely known.

FRENCH FRIES

Belgians eat a third more fries than Americans, per capita. In fact, the country is home to the Frietmuseum, a museum dedicated to the history and culture of French fries, based in the city of Bruges.

The longest curly fry measured thirty-eight inches, created at an Arby's in Asheville, North Carolina. Unlike many holders of food records, this one seems to have been created unintentionally and was discovered by a customer when it ended up in her order. She described the experience as "fry-tastic."

GUM

The distinctive pink color of bubble gum was a result of serendipity. Walter Diemer, an employee at the Fleer baseball card company, developed a gum that blew firm, dry bubbles that created a more satisfying effect than the gums that they had been working with—but it was also colorless and drab. He decided an eye-catching color would help with its marketability so he grabbed the only dye he had on hand, bright pink. It proved to strike just the right note of fun and has remained the default color of chewing gum ever since.

The city of San Luis Obispo, California, is home to Bubblegum Alley, a 70-foot-long, 15-foot-high alleyway on which passersby have stuck their used chewing gum since the 1950s or the Second World War (depending on who you ask). It's attracted tourists and gum chewers for decades, but local shop owners have complained that it is "unsavory and disgusting," resulting in not one but two full cleanings and removals of all the gum in the 1970s. But the cleared walls didn't stick; people were popping their wads on the walls within days of the cleanings and there hasn't been another serious attempt to remove the gum since.

Chad Fell holds the record for largest gum bubble ever blown without using one's hands. In 2004, he blew a bubble that was 20 inches in diameter (50.8 centimeters) at Double Springs High School in Winston County, Alabama. But the record holder for the largest bubble ever blown remains Susan Montgomery Williams, who blew a bubble measuring 23 inches (58 centimeters) in diameter in 1994. She did use her hands to assist, but also claimed to be the *loudest* popper in the world. In 1989, she was cited at the Fresno Fair when her loud popping created a disturbance for those trying to enjoy an outdoor Smokey Robinson concert.

HUMMUS

Beginning in 2008, "hummus wars" broke out between Israel and Lebanon, in which debate raged over which culture could claim credit for the delicious snack made of smashed chickpeas flavored with tahini and lemon juice. Thankfully, this has been a nonviolent battle, with the Guinness World Record for largest serving of hummus serving as a proxy arms race as each country has raised the stakes, with Israel setting the record with a 4,000-kilogram bowl in January 2010, only to lose four months later as three hundred Lebanese chefs created a 10,452-kilogram mountain of the stuff. The Association of Lebanese Industrialists petitioned Lebanese officials to request protected status from the European Commission to recognize hummus as uniquely Lebanese, and also sued marketers in Israel for promoting hummus as its own. Though the debate quieted down, it looks unlikely to ever fully go away. When Israel attempted to reclaim the title with a fifteen-ton plate of hummus in 2015, Guinness World Records actually declined to judge it out of concerns for the security of their judges.

NACHOS

Though these days you find nachos loaded with ingredients, the original just consisted of fried corn tortilla chips covered with melted cheese and sliced jalapeño peppers. No beef, beans, or any other fancy toppings were to be found. Chef Ignacio "El Nacho" Anaya, is credited with inventing the dish in 1940 when a customer asked if he could create a snack for them that was different than the restaurant's usual. He tossed the ingredients together and created a culinary phenomenon.

Of course, chefs have gotten far more creative with Anaya's basic nacho template since. The 2013 cookbook *Ultimate Nachos* includes recipes such as "Sage Brown Butter Artichoke Nachos," "Reuben Nachos" (with sauerkraut, Swiss cheese, and roast beef), and "Strawberry, Basil, and Mascarpone Dessert Nachos." Definitely a far cry from the simple chips, cheese, and jalapenos Anaya invented.

While Anaya is generally credited as the inventor of the dish, his family has not been able to profit from it beyond the bragging rights. In 1960, Ignacio Anaya Jr. sought out legal advice to help his father claim ownership over his increasingly popular appetizer.

"He said there's not much you can do after seventeen years. It's in the public domain," Anaya Jr. told the *South Florida Sun-Sentinel*.

PEANUT BUTTER

 Peanut butter used to be made with Spanish and Virginia peanuts. Today, it's more likely to be made with runner peanuts.

Two peanut farmers have been elected president of the United States: Georgia's Jimmy Carter and Virginia's Thomas Jefferson.

Some brands of peanut butter used to contain so much glycerin (used to keep the oil from separating) that the FDA had to formally require that for manufacturers to call their product "peanut butter," it must contain 90 percent peanuts.

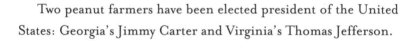

Arachibutyrophobia is the fear of peanut butter sticking to the roof of your mouth.

According to the National Peanut Board, the average twelve-ounce jar of peanut butter requires around 540 to 550 peanuts to fill.

POPCORN

In the popcorn industry, unpopped kernels are known as "old maids."

Food scientists at Purdue University solved the conundrum of "popability," discovering how to identify kernels that were more likely to pop before they were heated. In a 2005 study, the scientists found that the more "poppable" kernels actually had a stronger outer hull (known as the "pericarp"). This casing works as a natural pressure cooker, and as the moisture inside the kernel rises, forces it to burst into a satisfying puff. Those kernels with weaker hulls allow the moisture to escape without creating a full pop.

Popcorn was a key ingredient in many Aztec ceremonies. In the sixteenth century, Franciscan missionary Bernardino de Sahagún described how "a number of young women danced, having so vowed, a popcorn dance. As thick as tassels of maize were their popcorn garlands. And these they placed upon the girls' heads."

Another early Spanish account of an Aztec ceremony states how "they scattered before him parched corn, called momochitl, a kind of corn which bursts when parched and discloses its contents and makes itself look like a very white flower; they said these were hailstones given to the god of water."

POTATO CHIPS

That air in potato chip bags is not just there to make you wonder why they couldn't have filled the thing with chips. It serves as a cushion to help prevent the snacks from getting crunched. Also, that air is not oxygen, which can cause the snack to go bad—it's nitrogen, which helps maintain the chips' freshness.

There is a brand of chips known as The Whole Shabang that is oddly exclusive. Manufactured by The Keefe Group, the specially seasoned chips are sold exclusively in American prisons. While "prison chips" might not sound particularly appetizing, these snacks have earned a cult following from ex-cons and others who have had the chance to try them—with many seeking them out on eBay, writing about them on social media and message boards, and otherwise spreading the word about their crunchy deliciousness.

Speaking of unusual chip brands, Fail Chips, launched in 2017, offer a bag of tiny crushed-up bits of potato chips. Available in the flavors jalapeño, salt and vinegar, and barbecue, they're the perfect snack for those who love those end bits of chip at the bottom of the bag.

The first kind of flavored chip was barbecue.

The University of South Florida's Professor William E. Lee has spent decades studying salty snacks. Among his findings: "crunchy" chips that produce loud sounds at a low pitch and remain hard after 10 chews or more, result in more enjoyment by the eater than "crispy" chips that last only a few bites at a higher pitch.

TORTILLA CHIPS

The United Kingdom might not be known for its Mexican food, but in 2012, workers at British pub-grub restaurant chain Brewers Fayre baked the largest tortilla chip in the world. Weighing in at 110 pounds, it was thirty-two square feet in size, and required six people to move it. No word on how much guacamole accompanied it.

In 1994, Doritos revamped its chips to make them less dangerous. A $50 million investment from parent company PepsiCo not only gave the chips stronger flavors and made them both 15 percent thinner and 20 percent larger, but rounded the triangles' corners to dull the sometimes sharp points the tortilla chips had featured until that point, which could occasionally cause discomfort for those popping them too quickly into their mouths.

WALNUTS

Walnuts are the oldest tree foods known to man, dating back to 7000 BCE.

The most walnuts crushed by hand in one minute is 284, by Muhammad Rashid in Karachi, Pakistan, on July 15, 2018. Less than four months later, the same guy broke the record for most walnuts cracked with a head in one minute: 254.

YOGURT

Yogurt is far more popular with women than men (one survey found that 68 percent of women eat yogurt while just 43 percent of men do). However, guys may want to add some more of the stuff to their diets. An MIT study found that male mice that were fed yogurt inseminated their partners faster and produced larger litters than those that were not fed the milk products. Not only that, they ended up with testicles about 5 percent larger than the group that did not eat the yogurt, and 15 percent larger than those that were fed junk food.

> The Oxford English Dictionary recognizes at least a dozen spellings of the word, including "yoghurt," "yogurd," "yahourt," "yahourth," and "joghourt."

CHAPTER 6

SPICE UP YOUR LIFE

Unexpected morsels about your favorite condiments, sauces, and spices

 ## CINNAMON

Cinnamon has been found to prevent mold from growing. However, rather than requiring you to turn all your bread into cinnamon toast, a team of scientists developed an alternative solution: treating wax-paper packaging with cinnamon oil. In an experiment, they found the cinnamon-treated packaging inhibited 96 percent of mold growth thanks to the antimicrobials it produced.

Cinnamon was considered a precious spice and burned in funeral pyres in ancient Rome as a tribute to the gods (and to help cover up the unpleasant smell of burning flesh). Legend has it that Emperor Nero, who felt like he had to atone for his role in the death of his second wife, gathered up as much cinnamon as he could collect—compiling more than a year's worth of the stuff, which all went up in cinnamon-scented smoke.

HONEY

Not all honey is made by bees. The Mexican honey wasp produces large amounts of the sticky sweet stuff and proliferates throughout southern Texas as well as Mexico. The entire comb is eaten with the wasp larvae still in it and is considered a delicacy in Mexico, Brazil, and beyond.

Honey producer Clovermead holds an annual Bee Beard Competition in Ontario, Canada, in which contestants attract bees to swarm their bodies, while a partner "grooms" them into a beard shape.

HOT SAUCE

New Mexico State University is home to the Chile Pepper Institute. Established in 1992, the institution aims to build on the research of chile peppers begun when famed horticulturalist Fabian Garcia (dubbed "the father of the US chile pepper industry") began standardizing chile pepper varieties in 1888. Among the work it does is test the spice of some of the world's hottest peppers, measured in Scoville heat units (SHUs). The current top ten hottest peppers the CPI has tested and their approximate heat measurement (for comparison, jalapenos are up to 8,000 SHUs) are:

1. Trinidad Moruga Scorpion (2 million SHU)
2. Chocolate 7 pot (1.8 million SHU)
3. Trinidad Scorpion (1.5 million SHU)
4. Bhut Jolokia (1 million SHU)
5. Red 7 Pot (780,000 SHU)
6. Chocolate Habanero (700,000 SHU)
7. Red Savina Habanero (500,000 SHU)
8. Scotch Bonnet (350,000 SHU)
9. Orange Habanero (250,000 SHU)
10. Rocoto (175,000 SHU)

There are only two mammals that enjoy spicy foods: Humans . . . and the Chinese tree shrew. A study by Chinese researchers found that these little critters possess a mutation in their ion channel receptor, TRPV1, which makes them less sensitive to the "hot" chemical in chili peppers. The result is that in the test, the little rodents gobbled up corn pellets laced with capsaicin (the compounds that give peppers their spice) while other mammals avoided them.

There's a nineteenth-century opera about Tabasco sauce. First performed in 1894, *Burlesque Opera of Tabasco* tells the story of a

Turkish officer who, so frustrated by the lack of spice in his food, threatens to kill his French chef, who searches the city for spices to satisfy the officer. A blind beggar passes him a "secret potion" that proves just the right piquant flavor to save the chef's neck. That potion turns out to be a bottle of McIlhenny Company's own Tabasco brand pepper sauce. The company knew nothing about the performance when it was first written and staged, but eventually came to warmly endorse. The show was a hit at the time and is occasionally revived to fiery receptions.

KETCHUP

Ketchup was originally made from fish. While tomatoes are the main ingredient to this condiment today, the first recorded recipe of ketchup, dating back to 544 CE, urges the condiment maker to "take the intestine, stomach, and bladder of the yellow fish, shark and mullet, and wash them well. Mix them with a moderate amount of salt and place them in a jar. Seal tightly and incubate in the sun." Called "ke-tsiap," it was a popular sauce for Chinese sailors and was eventually discovered by the British, who anglicized it with the more familiar tomato.

The tomato-based condiment was generally written as "catsup" in the United States and throughout the West. It was Henry John Heinz and his brand of sauce that in the early 1900s opted to change the spelling to "ketchup," inspired by the original Chinese spelling and to set his product apart from competitors. The product took off and now "ketchup" is the default spelling in most areas.

Speaking of Heinz, that "57" on the label supposedly refers to the number of products the company sold, but when Henry came up with that branding device, it already sold well over sixty products. He just thought "57" was luckier—since his lucky number was five and his wife's was seven. The condiment's subsequent success seemed to validate his superstition.

MAYONNAISE

The origin of the word "mayonnaise" is hotly debated. One common story holds that the condiment was invented by the personal chef of a French admiral who in the 1756 Battle of Minorca, captured the city of Port Mahon—which provided the name's inspiration. However, others maintain that the sauce was stolen from the Catalan-speaking people of Minorca, who had already invented mayonnaise, calling it Salsa Mahonesa. Or it may have nothing to do with the battle, and simply be derived from *manier*, the French word for "to stir" or a confused translation referring to the French-Basque town of Bayonne. Like the condiment itself, the stories of its origin can prove divisive.

Mayonnaise is often recommended as a home remedy for defeating head lice. The theory is that a hefty mat of the oily condiment on one's scalp effectively suffocates both the nits and their eggs. While this is a popular home remedy, according to no less an authority than the Mayo Clinic, "This approach is rarely effective." They should know.

Mayo is actually less perishable than often believed. According to market research firm NPD Group, most commercially produced mayonnaise has a high enough acidity that it makes it difficult for bacteria that causes food-borne illnesses to grow. According to the company, "refrigerating commercial mayonnaise after opening has more to do with quality and extending its shelf life than it does with spoilage." The egg yolk used in its manufacturing is often pasteurized, as well. So, leaving it out overnight—or even for a few days—is not as dangerous to your health as is often claimed.

Mayo is the main ingredient in a number of sauces and dressings from aioli to remoulade to tartar sauce, but have you ever heard of *gribiche*? That's essentially a mayonnaise that's made with eggs that have been hard boiled rather than raw. Prepared with a bit of pickle and Dijon mustard, it's got a pleasantly piquant taste—but if you're going to order at a restaurant, first you'll have to figure out how to pronounce it.

MUSTARD

Most of the world's mustard is produced in Canada and Nepal. Seems like an odd pair, but both enjoy the temperate climates in which mustard seed thrives, with Canada producing 154 thousand metric tons of the stuff, followed by Nepal with 143 thousand metric tons.

Mustard is not actually yellow. That familiar color comes from the turmeric that is added to the condiment to round it out with an earthy, slightly bitter taste and eye-catching color. Mustard seed is actually a rather boring gray-brown color that would look much less appealing on a hot dog.

Middleton, Wisconsin, is home to the National Mustard Museum, which houses 6,090 mustards from all fifty US states and more than seventy countries. It also offers an expansive Mustard History exhibit and a collection of antique tins, mustard pots, and vintage advertisements—and, of course, a gift shop selling every type of mustard one can imagine.

SALAD DRESSING

Ranch dressing was invented by a cowboy. Well, when Kenneth Henson developed the recipe he was working as a contract plumber in Alaska for several years, refining the blend of buttermilk, salt, garlic, onion, herbs, and spices. However, when he and his wife set out to follow their dream of western living, they packed up and headed to Santa Barbara, California, and bought a 120-acre—you guessed it—ranch where they would host friends and family, with their signature dressing always close at hand. Eventually he started packaging the dry mix and trademarked his own Hidden Valley Ranch.

Disappointed in customers who would ask for a side of ranch to dip their pizza in, owner of Dallas pizzeria Il Cane Rosso mounted a bottle of the dressing to the wall in a glass case with the sign: "Side of Delicious Ranch Dressing $1,000.00." While the sign was meant as a joke, food-delivery company Caviar took the pizzeria up on the offer in 2016—donating $1,000 to the Humane Society of Southeast Texas in exchange for the side of ranch (the owner loves dogs as much as he hates ranch dressing). In March

2020, as the Covid-19 pandemic forced the restaurant to close its doors, none other than Hidden Valley Ranch itself stepped up and donated $2,000 to the pizzeria to help it during the difficult time—in exchange for two bottles of its own dressing.

SALSA

The company that made salsa a household name in the US was originally a syrup maker. Anyone familiar with salsa is probably aware of Pace Picante, which remains one of the top-selling salsa brands on the market. But before company founder David Pace started bottling and selling this "syrup of the Southwest," he had specialized in syrups, jams, and jellies. Eventually he started experimenting with ingredients and struck on the right combination of tomato, onion, and chile peppers that would appeal to American palates and had enough success that he discontinued his other products.

According to the US Department of Agriculture, salsa is a vegetable. The department determined in 1998 that the sauce could count as a veggie when included in school lunches. However, after getting heat when a push had been made to give ketchup the same designation in the early 1980s, the USDA determined that it only counts if the sauce is made with real vegetables—plenty of tomato, onion, and pepper—rather than a thin taco sauce or something mainly made of questionable ingredients such as food starches and gums.

"Pico de gallo" translates to "rooster's beak." While this is an odd name for this mix of chopped tomato, onion, Serrano peppers, and spices, the name refers to how the sauce is traditionally eaten: with one's finger and thumb, creating a quick-picking action that can look something like a rooster pecking for food.

SOY SAUCE

A study by researchers from the National University of Singapore found that Chinese dark soy sauce contains ten times the antioxidants of red wine and contributed to a decrease in risk of cardiovascular disease.

CHAPTER 7
STRANGE SIPS

*Odd bits about beverages
and libations*

 BEER

The Czech Republic consumes more beer per capita than any other country in the world (143.3 liters per person per year, on average). The country is followed by Namibia (108 liters), Austria (106 liters), Germany (104.2 liters), and Poland (100.8 liters).

According to the United States' Alcohol and Tobacco Tax and Trade Bureau, in 1983, there were forty-nine breweries in operation. At the end of 2019 there were 6,400 reporting brewers. So . . . beer's definitely gotten more diverse.

There are really only two types of beer. While you can find hundreds of styles at fancy grocery stores or snooty microbreweries, all beers fall into two basic categories: lagers and ales. These two are distinguished according to how yeast ferments during the brewing process. Ales are brewed at warmer temperatures with a top-fermenting yeast. Lagers are brewed at colder temperatures using bottom-fermenting strains of yeast. That's pretty much the only fundamental difference.

> In the 1960s, Heineken experimented with rectangular bottles, meant to double as bricks that could interlock with other Heineken bottles after being consumed—providing inexpensive building materials to low-income regions while reducing waste. About fifty thousand of these Heineken World Bottles, or WOBOs, were produced, but were never released commercially.

The strongest beer in the world is "Snake Venom," brewed by Scottish brewery Brewmeister. "Beer" is hardly an accurate word to describe it, though, considering the drink has an alcohol-by-volume level of 67.5 percent. That insane level of potency is produced through a process known as "freeze concentration" that pushes up the booziness.

The world's oldest continuously operating brewery is Weihenstephan Abbey, a Benedictine monastery in Weihenstephan, now part of Bavaria, Germany. Producing wheat beer, the brewery shares its site with the University of Munich's Faculty of Brewing Science and Beverage Technology, where students learn the brewing process and learn about microbiological principles of yeast and lactic acid bacteria.

When Danish physicist Niels Bohr won the Nobel Prize in Physics for his investigations into the structure of atoms, Denmark's Carlsberg brewing company gifted him a house with a pipeline going directly to the brewery, providing him free beer for life. The generous gift was not only a show of national pride, it was a symbol of the importance that the brewery put on science (it was in Carlsburg's on-site laboratory that *Saccharomyces pastorianus*, the species of yeast used to brew pale lagers, was first isolated).

COFFEE

Instant coffee might seem like a twentieth-century innovation, but in fact, the product dates back to the late eighteenth century. The first instant coffee is believed to have been launched in England in 1771, in which a patent for a "coffee compound" was granted by the British government. The first instant coffee to appear in the US did not arrive until 1851, and it took off during the Civil War as it was turned into experimental "cakes" that were shared in rations to soldiers.

> The people of Finland drink more coffee per capita than the citizens of any other country in the world—an average of 12 kilograms each annually, according to the International Coffee Organization. This is followed by Norway (9.9kg), Iceland (9kg) and Denmark (8.7kg).

Coffee has not always been beloved throughout Scandinavia. In 1746, the Swedish government banned both coffee and tea due to "the misuse and excesses of tea and coffee drinking," as the royal edict stated. Not only was the drink itself banned but also "coffee paraphernalia"—confiscating the cups and dishes out of which the stimulating drink was enjoyed. King Gustav III, concerned about public health and the drink's effect on individuals, ordered an experiment on a pair of identical twin brothers imprisoned for life: One was ordered to drink three pots of tea per day, the other to drink three pots of coffee. If the coffee drinker died first, it would demonstrate the drink's ill effects on one's health. In fact, it was Gustav who died first, assassinated in 1792. At least he wasn't around to find out the result of his experiment: The tea drinker was the first to go.

The most expensive coffee in the world comes from animal poop. Kopi luwak, made from coffee beans that have been partially digested by the catlike, long-tailed Indonesian creatures known as civets, can cost as much as $80 for a cup. The civets' digestive enzymes impact the structure of proteins in the coffee beans, removing their acidity and creating a distinctly smooth cup of java. However, the high demand for this distinctive drink has led to the animals being turned into tourist attractions, confined to cages on coffee plantations and given a diet of only coffee beans— resulting in malnutrition and sores from the wire cages in which they're kept. So, as fun as drinking poop coffee might seem, it might be both the financially wise and humane choice to stick with a more traditionally produced cup of joe.

Brewed coffee contains more caffeine than espresso. While a thick, potent ristretto might seem to pack a significantly more powerful punch than a standard Americano, in fact, according to the United States Department of Agriculture, brewed coffee contains one third more caffeine content (96 milligrams per serving) than an espresso (64 milligrams per serving). Of course, a "serving" of brewed coffee is 8 ounces, while a "serving" of espresso is just 1 ounce, but still.

While too much coffee can cause headaches, dizziness, and other unpleasant side effects, coffee is generally pretty good for you. Various studies have credited coffee with helping burn fat, lower one's risk for type 2 diabetes, and even protect a drinker from Alzheimer's disease and dementia. So drink up—responsibly.

EGGNOG

It might seem like the only thing dangerous about this beverage is the nausea that it brings on after more than a glass, but in 1826, the holiday drink was responsible for what came to be known as the Eggnog Riot. On Christmas Eve at West Point, cadets (who were prohibited from drinking) smuggled liquor into the free-flowing eggnog. As the party continued into the early morning, the drunken cadets grew increasingly rambunctious, running through the halls and wreaking havoc. Furniture was smashed, guns were fired, two officers were assaulted, and the school's commandant finally showed up and shut things down. Nineteen cadets were eventually court-martialed and sentenced to be dismissed from the academy. Talk about a holiday hangover.

 ## HOT CHOCOLATE

Hot chocolate has not always been sweet. The Mayans and Aztecs traditionally drank a lukewarm beverage called "xocoatl," made with chilies, water, and toasted corn. The arrival of Spanish Conquistadors transformed the beverage as they found it unpalatable and added sugar, cinnamon, and other sweeteners.

> Hot chocolate was sort of the original energy drink. Xocoatl was prized by the Aztecs and Mayans for its mood-boosting, energy-enhancing effects. Aztec leader Montezuma II was said to guzzle the stuff as a way to pump up his power and virility.

We're familiar with coffeehouses, but in seventeenth- and eighteenth-century England, it was "chocolate houses" that were all the rage. These members-only establishments served up hot chocolate in porcelain and silver pitchers to a crowd of boisterous gentlemen as they gambled, talked politics, and exchanged gossip. The hot, sweet drink was considered exotic at the time and attracted the city's elite and extravagant. Starbucks has nothing on these spots.

Hot chocolate might seem more like a treat these days, but it was once viewed as a sort of medicine. During the Revolutionary War, medics served up hot chocolate to wounded soldiers, believing it would help speed their recoveries. Incidentally, Thomas Jefferson was a major advocate of the drink, writing to John Adams in 1785 that "The superiority of chocolate, both for health and nourishment, will soon give it the preference over tea and coffee in America."

According to researchers at Cornell University, hot chocolate contains more antioxidants than red wine or tea. Although, since the drink is usually enjoyed with dairy and sugar that negate the health benefits, it's not typically viewed as a particularly healthy beverage.

ICED TEA

Iced tea helps spur the popularity of tall glasses. In the early part of the twentieth century, "iced tea glasses," purchased with long stirring spoons and small forks that could spear lemons became must-own accessories for the beverage.

LEMONADE

Why is lemonade so refreshing? Science! Japanese researchers in the 1960s found that more than any other flavor, sour tastes activate the salivary glands. This burst of moisture in the mouth caused by the acidity creates the satisfying sense of hydration. This is why lemonade really hits the spot—and why high levels of acidity tend to make for satisfying beverages in general (vinegar water was once a popular beverage in the US, and even Coca-Cola carries a surprisingly high level of acidity—about the same amount as vinegar—that balances its sweetness).

The police shut down a kids' lemonade stand in the city of Overton, Texas, in 2015 because the girls running it didn't have a permit to sell their fifty-cent refreshments. Authorities agreed to waive the permit fee of $150 as long as they got approval from the health department, including an inspection of their mom's kitchen. The girls responded by setting up the stand the next weekend, offering free lemonade, with donations welcome.

Partly due to stories like this, lemonade brand Country Time launched Legal-Ade in 2018, promising it would pay up to $300 in legal fees for each young lemonade-stand operators who had to foot the bill for permits—up to $60,000 total, if there were enough young entrepreneurs in need. "Life doesn't always give you lemons, but when it does, you should be able to make and share lemonade with the neighborhood without legal implications," Legal-Ade wrote on its website. "That's why we're here to take a stand for lemonade stands across the nation." Protests of requiring permits for lemonade stands even briefly inspired a Lemonade Freedom Day.

In the United States during the nineteenth century, lemonade was a popular alternative to alcohol among temperance advocates, with Sunkist even promoting its lemonade with the slogan, "Good-bye to liquor, here's to lemonade." When alcohol was banned at all state dinners and other functions by President Rutherford B. Hayes, his teetotaling wife earned the nickname "Lemonade Lucy."

Pink lemonade originated in the circus—at least that's where the two most widely circulated origin stories trace it back to. One legend has it that Henry E. Allott, who ran away to the circus in his teens, inadvertently invented pink lemonade when he dropped red-colored cinnamon candies in a tank of traditional lemonade he'd been preparing. Not wanting to waste good lemonade, he decided to pass off the colorful concoction as a new type of beverage. Another, grosser story holds that a lemonade seller (and brother of the circus lion tamer) ran out of water and in a pinch, decided to use the just-used bath water of one of the acrobats who had been wearing red tights. He branded it "strawberry lemonade" and sales doubled.

LIQUEUR

There are 40,000 cows across 1,500 farms dedicated to producing the cream that goes into Baileys Irish Cream. These bovines produce fifty million gallons each year to help produce enough bottles to meet demand for the highest-selling liqueur brand in the world.

The exact ingredients of Chartreuse, the naturally green French liqueur first developed by monks and dating back to the seventeenth century, remain a secret. According to the company that produces the drink, only two monks at the Grand Chartreuse monastery know the precise mix of 130 herbs and plants that go into the beverage.

Amaretto may taste like almonds, but most brands are actually made from the pits of apricots and peaches.

MILK

Twenty US states consider milk to be their official state beverage (Alabama's is whiskey).

A study by researchers at Britain's Newcastle University found that farmers who called their cows by name yielded an average of 268 more liters per cow than those who did not speak to them on a first-name basis. "Just as people respond better to the personal touch, cows also feel happier and more relaxed if they are given a bit more one-to-one attention," said Catherine Douglas of the School of Agriculture, Food, and Rural Development at Newcastle University. "What our study shows is what many good, caring farmers have long since believed."

Another surprising milk study: Those who drink whole milk were less likely to be obese than those who drank low-fat milk. A team of Swedish researchers looked at more than 1,700 men over a period of twelve years, and found that those who consumed high-fat milk, butter, and cream were significantly less likely to become obese over that time than those who drank the low-fat alternative.

A Russian folk belief holds that putting a frog in a bucket of milk helps to keep it from spoiling. While it's not clear what inspired this notion, recent research on frogs' skin secretions led by Moscow State University chemist A.T. Lebedev has found the amphibians carry high levels of peptides—antimicrobial compounds that serve as potent antibiotics against bacterial diseases such as Salmonella and Staphylococcus.

Of course, cows aren't the only animal that produces milk that humans can consume. A number of non cow milk products are available—though some you are only going to find at highly specialized stores. Some of the more unsavory sounding include:

- water buffalo gelato
- moose cheese
- reindeer cheese
- kumis (an alcohol made from fermented horse cheese, popular in Central Asia)
- human cheese (that's right—chefs and food engineers have experimented with creating cheese from human breast milk; it apparently has a mild taste and bouncy texture that is kind of gross)

SODA

Pepsi was originally named "Brad's Drink." New Bern, North Carolina drugstore owner Caleb Bradham concocted the fizzy beverage in his store and began selling it in 1893 under that name. To help explain just what Brad's Drink was, he changed the name five years later to a variation on "Pepsis," (the Greek word for "digestion"), which he claimed the beverage would aid, and the kola nut he used to flavor it—hence, Pepsi-Cola.

While Dr Pepper may not be the most popular soft drink, it is the oldest in America still on the market. In 1885 (a year before Coca-Cola made its debut), Waco, Texas pharmacist Charles Alderton noticed that visitors to his drug store combined a few—twenty-three, as legend has it—of the flavors being sold in his store's soda fountain to create a novel, fruity flavor. After a few adjustments, it proved a hit with the locals and was soon selling the syrup to other stores.

Dr Pepper was once promoted as a warm drink. For a few seasons in the 1960s, the soft drink's marketers advertised "Hot Dr Pepper," that is "delicious served steaming hot" over a thin slice of lemon. It caught on for a few years in the Southern US as a holiday beverage but eventually returned to its cooler roots.

If that doesn't sound weird enough, in the late 1980s, Coca-Cola's marketers ran a "Coke in the Morning" campaign that urged consumers to get their morning energy boost from the soda, rather than coffee. One of the advantages the company's spokespeople pointed to: Coke is less likely to spill in the lap of a morning commuter than a hot cup of coffee, and is a lot less painful when it does.

Fanta was created in Nazi Germany. Due to a trade embargo of the country during World War II, ingredients for Coca-Cola (including sugar) were difficult for Germans to source, so the head of Coca-Cola Deutschland came up with an alternative recipe that relied only on ingredients available in Germany at the time—including beet sugar, whey, and apple pomace. While it was invented in Germany during the war, it was not *invented by* Nazis, as it sometimes is erroneously accused of.

There are only two countries in the world where Coca-Cola is not sold: Cuba and North Korea.

SPIRITS

Sailors in the British Royal Navy used to receive a daily rum ration (known as a "tot") of half a pint in order to stay hydrated on long-haul travels. The amount was eventually reduced, but the practice continued all the way until 1970 as more sober minds won out and officers grew fed up with drunken sailors—particularly those getting drunk at the Queen's expense. July 31, 1970, the final day the rations were issued, became known as Black Tot Day.

James Bond may be clear about how he wants his martini prepared (shaken, not stirred), but he's more agnostic when it comes to what goes in it: Throughout Ian Fleming's novels, the secret agent orders nineteen vodka martinis and sixteen gin martinis.

Frank Sinatra was buried with a bottle of Jack Daniel's whiskey.

A team of researchers at the National Autonomous University figured out how to turn tequila into diamonds. The scientists were experimenting with how to create ultrathin films of diamond using organic solutions when they realized what worked best—40 percent alcohol and 60 percent water—was similar to the proportions in tequila. One of the researchers picked up a bottle of the spirit and they tested out heating it to 800 degrees Celsius, which produced a layer of carbon with crystal structures identical to diamonds. Unfortunately, these diamonds only measured about one thousandth of a millimeter across, making them far too small for jewelry.

TEA

The biggest consumer of tea in the world is Turkey—per capita, that is. The residents of Turkey sip an average of 6.96 pounds of tea every year. That's far more than the next-highest tea consumer, Ireland, where the citizens drink an average of just 4.83 pounds of tea a year. As a country overall, China is the biggest tea-drinker, consuming 1.6 billion pounds a year. However, broken down into per capita average, that adds up to just 1.29 pounds per person—making it the nineteenth-greatest consumer of tea the world, per capita.

The tea bag may have been invented by accident. Early in the twentieth century, American tea importer Thomas Sullivan shipped samples of his product in small silk pouches that customers were meant to empty into their tea pots to steep. When a number of customers asked for more tea in those convenient pouches so they could pop them directly into their hot water, Sullivan knew he had stumbled on to a great idea.

When tea grew in popularity in eighteenth-century England, there was not enough to meet the growing demand, leading to a rise in something called "smouch." It was a counterfeit tea that swapped out actual tea leaves for cheaper imitations such as ash and licorice leaves, dyed green or black. It led to the British government passing a 1725 act condemning smouch as causing "the ruin of the fair trader."

Darjeeling tea is sometimes referred to as the "Champagne of tea" due to the fact that, like that bubbly beverage, it must be grown in a specific region to earn its name. The Tea Board of India designates that "Darjeeling tea" can refer only to leaves that have been cultivated, manufactured, and processed in tea gardens of certain hilly areas in the District of Darjeeling in the State of West Bengal, India, and administers a Darjeeling mark and logo to designate legitimate Darjeeling." Though about ten thousand metric tons of the tea is produced in the region, the India Tea Board estimates four times that is sold as "Darjeeling tea" throughout the world annually.

> The namesake of Earl Grey tea, Charles Grey, prime minister of the United Kingdom from 1830 to 1834, helped bring about the abolition of slavery throughout the British Empire.

While the British famously love their tea, the drink has been steadily losing ground to coffee in recent years. A survey by the UK's Department for Environment, Food & Rural Affairs found that the average amount of tea purchased per person per week dropped from 30 grams in 2006 to 24 grams in 2015, while coffee rose from 17 grams to 21 grams in the same period. A 2017 survey conducted by syrup makers Monin even found that 61 percent of Brits say they actually prefer coffee to tea.

The Sky Kingdom religious sect in Malaysia became known as the "Teapot cult" after it constructed a two-story high, pink teapot meant to symbolize water's purity and "love pouring from heaven." It was accompanied by a giant vase into which the "holy water" poured from the teapot, which new followers would drink upon arrival to the commune.

World War II led to the virtual disappearance of green tea in the US. As the importing channels for tea sourced from China and Japan were closed off, Americans had to rely on the black tea sourced from India through England.

As it happens, the second-largest government purchase by the British government, by weight, in 1942 was tea—just after bullets and before artillery shells, bombs, and explosives. This was not just because the British consumed a lot of tea in a given year (though they did), but because the beverage was so fundamental to the British identity that any disruption in its availability was feared could severely damage national morale.

WINE

The world's oldest bottle of wine dates back as far as 325 CE Known as the "Speyer wine bottle," it was discovered in the tomb of a fourth-century Roman nobleman in 1867 near the city of Speyer, Germany. The tomb actually contained six glass bottles and ten vessels, but this was the only one that still contained liquid. Currently housed at the Historical Museum of Palatinate, it would not be very appealing to drink: It is about one-third full of clear liquid and the rest is a thicker resin substance that would be far from pleasant drinking. Plus, analyses have found that while part of the liquid was wine at one time, there is no longer any alcohol left.

While the Speyer wine bottle is the oldest known wine that is still liquid, shards of pottery jars have been discovered in the Republic of Georgia that contain remnants of wine dating back to 6000 BCE. The researchers found traces of four acids that would only be found in grape wine—though no pigments were found, making it impossible to say whether the wine had been red or white.

Prince Charles has a car that runs on wine. Engineers modified his vintage Aston Martin so that it could run on an alternative fuel made from a mixture of whey and a surplus of English white wine (technically, bioethanol, a fuel additive that's derived from wine, as well as other sources). He claimed it "runs better and is more powerful on that fuel than it is on petrol." Of course, England is not known for its wine—who knows how well it would run with a fine French vintage.

While water fountains are a common sight in most places, the small Italian town of Caldari di Ortona, in Abruzzo has significantly upgraded things, thanks to its very own public wine fountain. Installed at the Dora Sarchese Vineyard, the fountain's faucet, housed in a giant wine cask, spews out locally produced wine around the clock, for any visitor who pops a cup under the tap.

"Dumb wine" is a thing. That's the term used for wine that lacks odor, but may develop more of a "nose" over time, so it's seen as more of a phase than a permanent state of the wine. If a wine is odorless and wine experts expect that it is unlikely to ever develop much of a smell, then it's known as "numb wine."

A study published in the *Journal of Applied Psychology* found that the music played over the speakers in a supermarket could influence wine purchases. German and French music was played on alternating days over a two-week period. On the days that French tunes filled the store, more French wine sold, while the days of German music saw a rise in German wine sales.

In some parts of southeast Asia, you can buy "snake wine." A blend of rice wine and the blood and bile of a freshly killed venomous snake, it's neither particularly humane or tasty. However, it is believed to offer a range of medicinal benefits, such as improved circulation and relief of joint pain. One thing a drinker can be confident of: They won't be poisoned. The ethanol in the rice wine denatures the snake's venom and makes it harmless. Just because it won't kill you doesn't mean it's a good idea to drink it.

God saved wineries during Prohibition—at least, the Catholic Church did its part. When wine was outlawed in 1920, most winemakers were forced to close their doors, with one important exception: Those that produced sacramental wine used in Mass were allowed to continue. A number of wineries that continued putting out sacramental wine or adapted their offerings to appeal to this market survived the thirteen-year dry spell of Prohibition and made it out with their barrels intact.

Greek philosopher Plato suggested that wine should only be enjoyed in moderation for those up to age thirty and that "the young must abstain completely from drunkenness and from drinking large quantities of wine." Once a person reaches age forty, however, Plato urged that the wine should flow generously as it makes one feel young again and serves as a "remedy for the crabbedness of old age."

CHAPTER 8

SWEET ENDINGS

Peculiar origins and info about beloved desserts

 ## CAKE

German chocolate cake has nothing to do with Germany. It was named after Anglo-American chocolate maker Samuel German, who developed the dark baking chocolate that served as a key ingredient in the recipe. A homemaker going by Mrs. George Clay came up with the dessert, which she called "German's Chocolate Cake." The possessive form was soon dropped and the cake has been thought to have roots in Germany ever since.

Birthday cakes began as tributes to the gods. In ancient Greece, worshippers of the goddess Artemis would honor her birthday with a cake of flour and honey on the sixth day of every month (that's right, when you're a goddess you get twelve birthdays a year). Historians have even found evidence that these cakes were topped with lighted candles meant to symbolize the moonlight, as Artemis was the god of the moon.

> While Trappist monks have long been celebrated for the beer they brew and sell, one monastery in Missouri has gone a sweeter direction. The monks of Assumption Abbey in the Ozark Mountains have developed a recipe for a rich, traditional fruitcake that can be purchased online at trappistmonks.com.

CANDY

Cotton candy was invented by a dentist. Intentionally or not, William Morrison no doubt helped ensure others in his profession continued drawing in plenty of customers. In 1897, he partnered with candy maker John C. Wharton and came up with the design for the cotton-candy machine, and it's been bringing kids cavities ever since. However, the inventive dentist also came up with a chemical process that purified the public drinking water for his native city of Nashville and wrote a number of children's books and advocated reading among the young, so on balance he seems to have done plenty more good than harm for the youth.

Pez dispensers originally had no heads. They also came in only one flavor: Peppermint (the name "Pez" comes from *pfefferminze*, the German word for the refreshing flavor). Originally marketed to adults, the wizards at the Pez Candy Company eventually struck on the idea that they could sell more by giving the dispensers a bit more character—starting with a Pop-Eye and exploding into hundreds more (the company has produced at least 1,500 unique characters since).

How many licks does it take to get to the center of a Tootsie Pop? It depends on who (or what) is doing the licking. A group of engineering students at Purdue University created a "licking machine" modeled after a human tongue, which took an average of 364 licks to get to the center. A team of chemical engineering doctorate students at the University of Michigan created their own machine, which took an average of 411 licks. Then there are those who tried to get to the bottom (ahem, center) of the mystery the old-fashioned way, by having people lick the pop. A controlled study at Bellarmine University found the average to be between 148 and 198 licks (depending on the flavor), while a group of junior high students at Swarthmore Junior High School reported an average of 144 licks. So, while there has been no definitive answer, we can say that man is faster than machine at getting to the Tootsie

CANDY BARS

Baby Ruth bars are technically not named after the famous pitcher. When Chicago entrepreneur Otto Schnering created the peanut-and-caramel chocolate bar, he knew having Babe Ruth's name attached to it would be a marketing coup—but considering how famous the Sultan of Swat was at the time, the two sides were unable to reach a financial agreement that would be satisfying for both sides. So Schnering came up with a sneaky solution: He claimed that the bar was named after President Grover Cleveland's daughter, Ruth (nicknamed "Baby"). Considering that "Baby" Ruth Cleveland had died seventeen years earlier due to diphtheria, she was hardly a household name at the time, but it apparently gave Schnering enough legal cover that he continued to offer this as the "real namesake" of the candy.

> Kit Kat takes the cake when it comes to strange flavors around the world. Nestle, which manufactures the bar, has actively worked to create local variations on the classic wafer bar from one country to another. These include: Raspberry, Apple, Wasabi, Purple Sweet Potato, Red Pepper, Sweet Bean Jelly, among many others. Fans of the chocolate version clearly could be more imaginative.

In the late aughts, both Nestle and Mars launched their own energy-bar versions of traditional bars. Nestle's Butterfinger Buzz came packed with eighty milligrams of caffeine (as much as you'd get from an eight-ounce Red Bull). The center was also a much darker orange—almost red—color than the light orange coloration of a traditional Butterfinger. Mars' Snickers Charged came with sixty milligrams of caffeine, as well as taurine and other B vitamins. Unsurprisingly, neither really caught on.

The record for largest chocolate bar by area is held by Dutch chocolatier Frits van Noppen, who led a team that created a massive bar measuring 4,125 square feet (383.24 square meters) to celebrate the company's twentieth anniversary. The massive bar featured an illustration of the new hospital ship of international charity Mercy Ships (with profits from the bar's sale going to the organization).

CARAMEL

Milton Hershey began his confectionary career not in chocolate, but in caramels. He started the Lancaster Caramel Company in 1886 in the city of Lancaster, Pennsylvania. His sweets caught on quickly—including ones covered in milk chocolate. When his workers figured out a way to prepare the ingredients for milk chocolate without burning them, it wasn't long before he began churning out the products that would make his name synonymous with chocolate.

Caramel apples were invented thanks to leftover Halloween candy. In the 1950s, Kraft Foods employee Dan Walker was considering ways to repurpose the loads of leftover chewy caramels the company had on hand after the surge of Halloween sales. He experimented with melting the sweets and dipping apples into it, and invented an iconic treat in the process. It would not be until 1960 that Chicago native VIo Raimondi came up with a way to automate the dipping, saving the candy makers from doing it all by hand.

CHOCOLATE

When it comes to indulgent desserts, it's hard to beat The Fortress Stilt Fisherman Indulgence. Created by the pastry chef at The Fortress Resort & Spa in Sri Lanka, it features an Italian cassata flavored with Baileys liqueur and is served with a pomegranate and mango compote attached to a handcrafted chocolate stilt fisherman. What's so fancy about that? One final ingredient puts it over the top: an eighty-carat aquamarine stone placed onto the chocolate sculpture. Altogether, the dessert costs $14,500.

Hershey's Kisses get their names from the smooching sound and motion the machine made when it popped the candy onto the conveyor belt. Introduced in 1907, the teardrop-shaped chocolates were originally wrapped by hand, but by 1921 the machine was engineered to wrap them automatically. We weren't able to confirm if that impacted the kissing sound.

The namesakes of M&Ms hated each other. Forrest Mars and Bruce Murrie, the businessmen who created the candy-coated chocolates, had a contentious relationship. In 1949, Mars managed to leverage Murrie out of his 20 percent share of Mars

Incorporated, which manufactured the chocolates—not long before M&Ms would go on to become the best-selling candy in the United States. Murrie received just $1 million for what would soon become a multibillion-dollar business.

COOKIES

Fig Newtons were not named after Sir Isaac Newton, as is often believed. In fact, they were named after the city of Newport, Massachusetts, where the cookie was created (well, *near* where the cookie was invented—technically it was created in the city of Cambridgeport in 1895, Fig Cambridgeport doesn't roll off the tongue nearly as well).

In 2018, Nabisco "released" the animals on the packaging of its Animal Crackers—after 116 years of depicting them in circus cages. The change came as a result of a criticism from the People for the Ethical Treatment of Animals, which complained that it reflected "exploitation of animals." The snack company saw PETA's point, and the label now features a zebra, elephant, lion, giraffe, and gorilla roaming free.

Cookie Monster began as a Potato Chip Monster. The character made its first public appearance in advertisements for Frito-Lay's Munchos chips, grabbing a bag of the crisps and devouring them with his signature intensity. At the time, Jim Henson dubbed him

Arnold, the Munching Monster, but he would be given a different snack of choice when Henson developed *Sesame Street* soon after.

DOUGHNUTS

Doughnuts originally were made without a hole in the center. First developed in Holland as *olykoek*, or "oil cake," the sweet pastry made its way to the US in the early seventeenth century. It would take another century and a half before Hanson Gregory, a sea captain in Maine, would reputedly come upon the idea of adding a hole, thereby increasing the surface area for frying and eliminating the soggy center.

Americans eat ten billion doughnuts a year, but Canada holds the distinction of most doughnut shops per capita—five times as many per capita as its southern neighbor. This is thanks in large part to beloved Canadian chain Tim Hortons, which has more than four thousand locations throughout the country.

ÉCLAIR

The word "éclair" means "flash of lightning" in French. It's debated whether it earned the name because of the way light reflects off the pastry's icing or because it disappears as fast as a lightning bolt when set on the table.

FORTUNE COOKIES

In 2005, 110 people all won the second prize in the Powerball lottery. Officials immediately suspected fraud had occurred (considering the number of tickets sold, just four or five winners would be the usual number expected). It turned out, the winners had gotten their numbers from fortune cookies produced in the same factory based in Queens, New York.

Fortune cookies are not really eaten in China. They were introduced by Chinese restaurants in California—many of which were owned by Japanese immigrants—and known as "fortune tea cakes" before spreading throughout the United States following World War II. Today, almost three billion fortune cookies are produced in the world, almost all of them in the United States.

GUMMIES

There's a jujube plant. The eponymous gummy candies got their moniker because they originally contained juice from fruits of the *Ziziphus jujuba* tree, found in India and China. The date-like fruits turn a dark red when ripe, and when dried serve as a sweet confection. However, today's Jujubes contain mostly corn syrup and flavorings.

ICE CREAM

Ben Cohen, cofounder of Ben and Jerry's Ice Cream, is anosmic—that is, he has no sense of smell and only a partial sense of taste. It was his lack of these senses that led him to urge partner Jerry Greenfield to add large chunks to their ice cream.

John Harrison, who for decades served as Dreyer's "Official Taste Tester" insured his tongue for $1 million and used a gold-plated spoon to make his way through the average of sixty samples he tried each day (claiming it did not leave the "slight resin aftertaste" left by plastic). How did a guy who tasted sixty spoonfuls of ice cream every day avoid packing on the pounds? As he explained to a writer for *Cooking Light*: "I swirl the ice cream around in my mouth to coat all the taste receptacles, and then I spit it out."

Mexico and Central America is home to the pacay tree, better known as the "ice-cream bean tree" because the pods it produces taste oddly similar to vanilla ice cream. Mexican coffee growers use the trees to shade their plants—and sell the pacay pods for an extra profit. They're usually eaten raw or roasted, with some sellers opening stalls outside of theaters, selling the snacks to moviegoers.

French ice-cream maker Philippe Faur has developed a foie gras ice cream, made from Armagnac, sugar, pepper and, of course, plenty of the fattened (and controversial) duck liver dish foie gras.

A UK-based creamery invented glow-in-the-dark ice cream. Charlie Francis, the entrepreneur behind the ice-cream company Lick Me I'm Delicious, added to his vanilla ice cream a jellyfish protein that causes it to glow and brighten in response to the warmth and higher pH level of the tongue. Even though it incorporates jellyfish, the fluorescent ice cream does not sting. It is not cheap either, costing 140£ (approximately $225) per scoop. Jellyfish protein ain't cheap!

MARSHMALLOWS

Marshmallows began as medicine. The mucilage (basically sap) from the marsh mallow plant that grows in European wetlands was a popular treatment for sore throats and coughs, usually mixed with sugar to make it palatable. In France, this was taken a step further, and the substance was whipped with egg and sugar to create lozenges and then a sweet gelatin. By the nineteenth century it made its way to the United States, where confectioners devised the recipe that allowed the foam to set in the traditional marshmallow form we recognize today. But while their soft, spongy form is more fun, modern marshmallows might not be quite so good as the original mucilage for relieving a cold.

MILKSHAKES

A milkshake almost killed Fidel Castro. One of the numerous assassination attempts made on the Cuban leader by the CIA was to have a restaurant worker at the Havana Libre Hotel that he frequented sneak poison into a chocolate milkshake—his preferred dessert when staying there. However, the plan was spoiled when the worker stored the pills in the freezer, where they froze, bursting when the conspirator grabbed them.

In Rhode Island, milkshakes are known as "cabinets." The name is believed to come from the fact that blenders were typically kept in small, wooden cabinets. (Technically, the "coffee cabinet" is a specific kind of milkshake, made by blending ice cream with the state's official beverage, coffee milk—a combination of coffee syrup and milk.) If you see "milkshakes" on the menu, it will be for a beverage that simply combines syrup and milk, shaken.

PIE

The pastime of Frisbee began with a pie. Beginning in the 1870s at Yale University, students would toss empty tins from the Frisbie Pie Company around campus, yelling "Frisbie!" The game quickly spread across campuses throughout the US. When the cofounders of the Wham-O toy company bought the rights to a similarly shaped "Pluto Platter" flying disc, devised by inventor Walter Frederick Morrison, they learned that college students still called the toy "Frisbie," they decided to capitalize on the name recognition, dubbing it "Frisbee."

POUND CAKE

Pound cake gets its name from the fact that the recipe calls for a pound each of flour, butter, eggs, and sugar.

TIRAMISU

Luca Parmitano, the first Italian astronaut to walk on the moon, requested a particular hometown treat for his landing in 2013. Turin chef Davide Scabin devised a special dehydrated version of tiramisu to give him a taste of home more than two hundred thousand miles away. (It capped off a meal of antipasto, lasagna, and eggplant Parmesan.)

Tiramisu may seem like a classic dessert that has been around for decades, if not longer. In fact, the first time the dessert's name appeared in print in Italian was 1980.

TWINKIES

Chicago bakery manager James Dewar came up with the idea for Twinkies as a way for his company to utilize the machines it used for creating strawberry shortcake snacks during the ten months of the year when strawberries weren't in season. Since bananas were in season year round, he realized creating a pound cake snack filled with banana cream could make an ideal alternative—and proved more correct than he could have dreamed.

Dewar lived to eighty-eight, and claimed he consumed his spongy sweets every day (along with half a pack of cigarettes). To those who called his concoction "junk food," he rebutted: "I fed them to my four kids, and they feed them to my fifteen grandchildren. My boy Jimmy played football for the Cleveland Browns. My other son, Bobby, played quarterback for the University of Rochester. Twinkies never hurt them."

WEDDING CAKE

Wedding cake began as something guests threw, rather than ate. In ancient Rome, guests would throw small wheat cakes at the married couple or crumble cake over the head of the bride as a symbol of fertility. Eventually, rice took the place of the projectile and the cake was left for eating.

CONCLUSION

Thanks for reading! I hope you found these facts to be odd, unexpected, and not *too* stomach turning. If there is one thing to take away from this compendium of curious culinary tidbits, it's that even those things you think you know well can still surprise you. Hope you learned something new, or at least worked up a bit of an appetite.

ABOUT THE
AUTHOR

Alex Palmer is a journalist and excavator of fascinating facts. He is the author of the original Weird-o-Pedia as well as books of surprising tidbits including *Happiness Hacks*, *Alternative Facts*, and *Literary Miscellany*. He is also the *New York Times* best-selling author of *The Santa Claus Man* and his writing has appeared in *Lifehacker*, *Best Life*, *Mental Floss*, *Slate*, and *Esquire*.

SOURCES

Chapter 1—Fresh Fruit: Sweet slices of info about your favorite fruits

APPLES

Bader, Myles H. *The Wizard of Food's Encyclopedia of Kitchen & Cooking Secrets*. Strategic Book Publishing, 2010, page 18.

Giles, Autumn. "The Science of Cold Apple Storage." *Modern Farmer*. August 5, 2013. https://modernfarmer.com/2013/08/the-science-of-cold-apple-storage/.

Chaussee, Jennifer. "Here's How Many Apple Cores It Would Take to Poison You." *Wired*. September 9, 2016. https://www.wired.com/2016/09/heres-many-apple-cores-take-poison/.

"Heaviest apple." Guinness World Records. https://www.guinness worldrecords.com/world-records/heaviest-apple?fb_comment_id= 762797713758193_1189688831069077.

APRICOTS

Denker, Joel. "'Moon of the Faith:' A History of the Apricot and Its Many Pleasures." The Salt. June 15, 2016. https://www.npr.org/sections/thesalt/2016/06/14/481932829/moon-of-the -faith-a-history-of-the-apricot-and-its-many-pleasures.

AVOCADOS

"What's in a name?" University of California Agriculture & Natural Resources. http://ucavo.ucr.edu/General/HistoryName.html.

Murray, Michael T., and Joseph Pizzorno. *The Encyclopedia of Healing Foods*. Simon & Schuster, 2010, page 255.

Verde, Isvett. "Avocado Dye Is, Naturally, Millennial Pink." *New York Times*. July 15, 2019. https://www.nytimes.com/2019/07/15 /fashion/avocado-dye-is-naturally-millennial-pink.htm.

BANANAS

Matthews, Robert. "Do apples really ripen faster if you put them next to bananas?" Science Focus. https://www.sciencefocus.com /nature/do-apples-really-ripen-faster-if-you-put-them-next-to -bananas/.

"10 Brilliant Uses For Banana Peels." *Prevention*. March 19, 2015. https://www.prevention.com/health/a20448896/life-hacks-using -banana-peels/.

BLACKBERRIES

"LifeSavers." Andrew Smith and Bruce Kraig, eds. *Oxford Encyclopedia of Food and Drink in America*. Oxford University Press. 2014, page 476.

"Blackberry, Bramble." Gabrielle Hatfield. *Encyclopedia of Folk Medicine*. ABC CLIO. 2004, page 33.

BLUEBERRIES

Lawson, Carol. "After a Protest by Parents, Crayola Changes Its Recipes." *New York Times*. November 15, 1995. https://www.nytimes. com/1995/11/15/garden/after-a-protest-by-parents-crayola -changes-its-recipes.html?n=Top/Reference/Times+Topics /Subjects/C/Children+and+Youth.

CHERRIES

Carroll, James R. "164 years ago, nation shocked by Zachary Taylor's sudden death, leaving a mystery behind." *Courier Journal*. July 8, 2014. https://www.courier-journal.com/story/politics-blog /2014/07/08/kentuckys-zachary-taylor-died-164-years-ago-amid -political-chaos/12355073/.

COCONUTS

Eschner, Kat. "Why JFK Kept a Coconut Shell in the Oval Office." *Smithsonian*. August 2, 2017. https://www.smithsonianmag.com

/smart-news/why-jfk-kept-coconut-shell-white-house-desk
-180964263/.

Silverman, Jacob. "How Napalm Works." *How Stuff Works.* https:
//science.howstuffworks.com/napalm.htm.

FIGS

Padmanaban, Deepa. "A tale of loyalty and betrayal, starring figs
and wasps." BBC Earth. May 1, 2016. http://www.bbc.com/earth
/story/20160429-a-tale-of-loyalty-and-betrayal-starring-figs
-and-wasps.

GRAPEFRUIT

"How did the grapefruit get its name? It doesn't look like a
grape." Everyday Mysteries, Library of Congress. https://www.loc
.gov/everyday-mysteries/item/how-did-grapefruit-get-its-name-it
-doesnt-look-like-a-grape/.

"Grapefruit Juice and Some Drugs Don't Mix." Food and Drug
Administration. https://www.fda.gov/consumers/consumer-updates
/grapefruit-juice-and-some-drugs-dont-mix.

GRAPES

Griffiths, James, and Junko Ogura. "This bunch of grapes just sold
for $11,000 in Japan." CNN. July 9, 2019. https://www.cnn.com
/travel/article/japan-grapes-expensive-fruit-intl-hnk/index.html/

"Twelve Grapes." Gastro Obscura. https://www.atlasobscura.com
/foods/twelve-grapes-new-years-eve.

KIWIS

Lui, Kevin. "This Kiwifruit Isn't from New Zealand at All. It's Chinese, and This Is How It Got Hijacked." *TIME*. February 8, 2017. https://time.com/4662293/kiwifruit-chinese-gooseberry-new-zealand-history-fruit/.

LEMONS

"Lemon juice experiment." BBC Science. September 17, 2014. http://www.bbc.co.uk/science/humanbody/mind/articles/personalityandindividuality/lemons.shtml.

"A New Fruit—Sweet Lemons." *Syracuse Herald*. December 12, 1928, 8.

LIMES

Karp, David. "Boom times for limes." *Los Angeles Times*. December 2, 2011. https://www.latimes.com/food/la-fo-marketwatch-20111202-story.html.

ORANGES

Soniak, Matt. "Which Came First: Orange the Color or Orange the Fruit?" *Mental Floss*. February 8, 2012. https://www.mentalfloss.com/article/29942/which-came-first-orange-color-or-orange-fruit.

PEACHES

Jampel, Sarah. "What Is a Donut Peach and Why Are They Everywhere Right Now?" *Bon Appetit*. August 18, 2018. https://www.bonappetit.com/story/what-is-a-donut-peach.

PEARS

Smith, Andrew F., ed. *Oxford Encyclopedia of Food and Drink in America,* Volume I. New York: Oxford University Press, 2004, page 530.

Dalby, Andrew. *Food in the Ancient World from A to Z.* London: Routledge, 2003, page 253.

PINEAPPLES

McCord, Garrett. "The Curious Flesh Eating Enzymes in Pineapple and Papaya." The Spruce Eats. September 21, 2019. https://www .thespruceeats.com/flesh-eating-enzymes-of-pineapple-and -papaya-4047013.

Black, Annetta. "World's Largest Plant Maze." Atlas Obscura. https: //www.atlasobscura.com/places/worlds-largest-plant-maze.

RASPBERRIES

Geggel, Laura. "Why Are Bananas Berries, But Strawberries Aren't?" Live Science. January 12, 2017. https://www.livescience.com /57477-why-are-bananas-considered-berries.html.

"Astronomers find Milky Way 'could taste of raspberries.'" *The Telegraph.* April 21, 2009. https://www.telegraph.co.uk/news /newstopics/howaboutthat/5191040/Astronomers-find-Milky -Way-could-taste-of-raspberries.html.

STRAWBERRIES

Myers, Vanessa Richins. "Those Aren't Seeds on the Outsides of Strawberries." The Spruce. January 12, 2020. https://www.thespruce .com/fruits-with-their-seeds-outside-3269379.

Cornford-Matheson, Alison. "Belgium's Strawberry Museum." AFAR. https://www.afar.com/places/musee-de-la-fraise-de-wepion-namur.

WATERMELONS

Krans, Brian. "4 Watermelon Rind Benefits." Healthline. September 16, 2019.

Chapter 2—Crisp and Curious: Nourishing facts about vegetables

ARTICHOKES

Brion, Raphael. "Doctor Sues Restaurant for Letting Him Eat a Whole Artichoke." Eater. November 17, 2010. https://www.eater.com/2010/11/17/6709697/doctor-sues-restaurant-for-letting-him-eat-a-whole-artichoke.

Morgan, Michelle. *Marilyn Monroe: Private and Confidential*. New York: Skyhorse Publishing, 2012, page 92.

ASPARAGUS

Briggs, Bill. "Psst: asparagus pee. Are you in the club?" NBC News. June 29, 2012. https://www.nbcnews.com/healthmain/psst-asparagus-pee-are-you-club-853260.

BEETS

Evans, Ben. "Partners in Space: 40 Years Since the Remarkable Voyage of Apollo-Soyuz (Part 2)." AmericaSpace. July 12, 2015.

BROCCOLI

Mattheis, Christine. "12 Foods with More Vitamin C than Oranges." ABC News. https://abcnews.go.com/Health/Wellness/12 -foods-vitamin-oranges/story?id=20729780.

Kovalchik, Kara. "Why Isn't There Canned Broccoli?" *Mental Floss.* January 8, 2014. https://www.mentalfloss.com/article/54426/why -isnt-there-canned-broccoli.

"'Definitely' is most commonly misspelt word." *The Telegraph.* June 15, 2009. https://www.telegraph.co.uk/education/educationnews /5538890/Definitely-is-most-commonly-misspelt-word.html.

Couch, Christina. "How to Raise a 165-Year-Old Cat." Atlas Obscura. December 15, 2015. https://www.atlasobscura.com/articles/how -to-raise-a-165-year-old-cat.

BRUSSELS SPROUTS

Nsubuga, Jimmy. "Man pushes Brussels sprout up Mount Snowdon using nose and it's all for charity." *Metro.* August 3, 2014. https: //metro.co.uk/2014/08/03/man-pushes-brussels-sprout-up -mount-snowdon-using-nose-and-its-all-for-charity-4820002/.

Ayto, John. *An A-Z of Food and Drink.* Oxford University Press, 2002, pages 44–45.

CARROTS

Subramanian, Sushma. "Fact or Fiction: Raw Veggies Are Healthier than Cooked Ones." *Scientific American.* March 31, 2009. https://www .scientificamerican.com/article/raw-veggies-are-healthier/.

"Can Eating Too Many Carrots Turn Your Skin Orange?" Cleveland Clinic. https://health.clevelandclinic.org/can-eating-too -many-carrots-turn-your-skin-orange.

Davidson, Alan. *Oxford Companion to Food.* Oxford: Oxford University Press, 1999, page 140.

CAULIFLOWER

Picht, Randolph. ""Orange Cauliflower! Not just a gimmick, hybrid could save farmers costly task of tying off leaves." *Chicago Tribune.* October 20, 1988.

CELERY

Rupp, Rebecca. "Sex and the Celery: Ancient Greeks Get Busy With Help From Veggies." *National Geographic.* May 20, 2014. https://www .nationalgeographic.com/culture/food/the-plate/2014/05/20 /sex-celery-ancient-greeks-get-busy-help-veggie/.

CORN

"Corn Facts." Iowa Corn Growers Association. https://www.iowacorn .org/media-page/corn-facts.

CUCUMBER

Waugh, Rob. "Here is the actual scientific reason cats are afraid of cucumbers." *Metro.* November 18, 2015. https://metro.co.uk /2015/11/18/here-is-the-actual-scientific-reason-cats-are-afraid-of -cucumbers-5509634/.

Boswell, James. *The Journal of a Tour to the Hebrides with Samuel Johnson, LL.D.*

EGGPLANT
Smith, Andrew F. *Oxford Encyclopedia of Food and Drink in America*. Oxford University Press, 2004, page 671.

GARLIC
Andrews, Tamra. *Nectar and Ambrosia: An Encyclopedia of Food in World Mythology*. Santa Barbara, California: SBC-CLIO, 2000, pages 99–100.

Sandvik, H., and A. Baerheim. "Does garlic protect against vampires? An experimental study." *Tidsskrift for den Norske laegeforening: tidsskrift for praktisk medicin, ny raekke* 114.30 (1994): 3583–3586.

KALE
O'Hagan, Lauren Alex. "Celebrity greens kale and seaweed were long considered food of last resort." The Conversation. November 21, 2019. https://theconversation.com/celebrity-greens-kale-and-seaweed-were-long-considered-food-of-last-resort-124663.

Butler, Carolyn. "Eat your kale." *Washington Post*. September 24, 2012. https://www.washingtonpost.com/national/health-science/eat-your-kale/2012/09/24/95a4d756-018f-11e2-9367-4e1bafb958db_story.html.

ONIONS
Kiple, Kenneth F., and Kriemhild Ornelas. The *Cambridge World History of Food*. Cambridge University Press, 2000, page 250.

POTATOES

Hiskey, Daven. "Why Are Potatoes Called Spuds?" *Mental Floss.* November 15, 2012. https://www.mentalfloss.com/article/13090 /why-are-potatoes-called-spuds.

PUMPKINS

Foster, Kelly. "What's Actually in Your Canned Pumpkin Purée?" The Kitchn. October 16, 2014. https://www.thekitchn.com /whats-actually-in-your-canned-pumpkin-puree-ingredient -intelligence-69123.

Barksdale, Nate. "The History of Pumpkin Pie." History.com. November 21, 2014. https://www.history.com/news/the-history-of -pumpkin-pie.

Taylor, Timothy. "The Dominance of Peoria in the Processed Pumpkin Market." BBN Times. November 23, 2018. https://www .bbntimes.com/global-economy/the-dominance-of-peoria-in -the-processed-pumpkin-market.

RADISHES

Staub, Jack. *75 Exciting Vegetables for Your Garden.* Layton, Utah: Gibbs Smith, 2005, page 59.

RHUBARB

Rupp, Rebecca. "Does Rhubarb Deserve Its Killer Reputation?" *National Geographic.* May 18, 2016. https://www .nationalgeographic.com/culture/food/the-plate/2016/05/18 /does-rhubarb-deserve-its-killer-reputation/.

SALAD

Gora, L Sasha. "The surprising truth about Caesar salad." BBC. May 22, 2019. http://www.bbc.com/travel/story/20190521-the-surprising-truth-about-caesar-salad.

Monaghan, Gail. "Screen Siren Cobb Salad." *Wall Street Journal.* June 26, 2011. https://www.wsj.com/articles/screen-siren-cobb-salad-11596116435.

Thiele, Rebecca. "World's Longest Salad Bar to be made in Hudsonville." WMUK. July 25, 2013. https://www.wmuk.org/post/worlds-longest-salad-bar-be-made-hudsonville#stream/0.

SAUERKRAUT

Leblanc, Tyler. "Magical Sour Cabbage: How Sauerkraut Helped Save the Age of Sail." *Modern Farmer*, April 23, 2014.

SPINACH

Shah, M. M. Enzymes for Degradation of Energetic Materials and Demilitarization of Explosives Stockpiles-SERDP Annual (Interim) Report, 12/98. No. PNNL-12081; 4015EM040. Pacific Northwest National Lab., Richland, WA (US), 1999.

Gershlak, Joshua R., et al. "Crossing kingdoms: using decellularized plants as perfusable tissue engineering scaffolds." *Biomaterials* 125 (2017): 13–22.

TOMATOES

Dewey, Caitlin. "The obscure Supreme Court case that decided tomatoes are vegetables." *Washington Post.* October 18, 2017.

https://www.washingtonpost.com/news/wonk/wp/2017/10/18/the-obscure-supreme-court-case-that-decided-tomatoes-are-vegetables/.

Smith, K. Annabelle, "Why the Tomato Was Feared in Europe for More than 200 Years." *Smithsonian*, June 18, 2013. https://www.smithsonianmag.com/arts-culture/why-the-tomato-was-feared-in-europe-for-more-than-200-years-863735/?no-ist.

YAMS

Fisher, Max. "Nigerian Sesame Street Subs Yams for Cookies." *The Atlantic*. August 25, 2010. https://www.theatlantic.com/international/archive/2010/08/nigerian-sesame-street-subs-yams-for-cookies/340224/.

Chapter 3—Fun with Flour: Surprising facts about breads, cereal, grains, and baked goods

BAGELS

Infante, John. "How the NCAA Banned Cream Cheese." Athnet. October 4, 2012. https://www.athleticscholarships.net/2012/10/04/how-ncaa-banned-cream-cheese.htm.

Balinska, Maria. *The Bagel: The Surprising History of a Modest Bread*. Yale University Press, 2008, page 46.

"Answers About the History of the Bagel." *New York Times*. September 2, 2009. https://cityroom.blogs.nytimes.com/2009/09/02/answers-about-the-history-of-the-bagel/.

BAGUETTE

Monaco, Emily. "The perfect French baguette." BBC Travel. August 26, 2019. http://www.bbc.com/travel/story/20190825-the -perfect-french-baguette.

BREAD ROLLS

"Free Bread: Bane or Boon?" *Restaurant Hospitality* (June 1, 2011): 1.

CEREAL

"Tony the Tiger: Mascot of Kellogg's Frosted Flakes." Retroplanet. June 19, 2008. https://blog.retroplanet.com/kelloggs-frosted-flakes -tony-the-tiger-mascot/.

"A Short History of Cereal." *New York Times*. February 22, 2016. https://www.nytimes.com/interactive/2016/02/22/dining /history-of-cereal.html.

CIABATTA

"The secret life of ciabatta." *The Guardian*. April 29, 1999. https: //www.theguardian.com/theguardian/1999/apr/30/features11.g24.

ENGLISH MUFFINS

Jaine, Tom, and Davidson, Alan. *The Oxford Companion to Food*. United Kingdom: OUP Oxford, 2014, page 535.

"Baker's Dozen." The Phrase Finder. https://www.phrases.org.uk /meanings/Bakers-dozen.html.

GRAHAM CRACKERS

Eveleth, Rose. "Graham Crackers Were Supposed To Be a Sex Drive–Suppressing Diet Food." *Smithsonian.* April 4, 2013. https://www.smithsonianmag.com/smart-news/graham-crackers-were-supposed-to-be-a-sex-drivesuppressing-diet-food-15675399/.

OATS

McCulloch, Stuart. *A Scion of Heroes.* United Kingdom: Troubador Publishing Limited, 2015, page 313.

Anderson, Jean. *The American Century Cookbook: The Most Popular Recipes of the 20th Century.* New York City: Clarkson Potter, 1997, page 482.

PIZZAS

Mariani, John F. *Encyclopedia of American Food and Drink.* New York: Lebhar-Friedman, 1999, page 244.

The Morning Post (December 17, 1860): 6.

Leroux, Charles. "Ike and Ric: They were first with the thickest." *Chicago Tribune Magazine* (August 1, 1976): 14.

PRETZELS

Esposito, Russell R. *The Golden Milestone: Over 2500 Years of Italian Contributions to Civilization.* New York City: New York Learning Library, 2000, page 134.

RICE

https://www.irri.org/international-rice-genebank.

"Is Throwing Rice at Weddings Bad for Birds?" Snopes.com. May 14, 2000. https://www.snopes.com/fact-check/against-the-grain/.

SANDWICH BREAD

Copeland, Libby. "White Bread Kills." *Slate*. April 6, 2012. https://slate.com/human-interest/2012/04/a-review-of-white-bread-a-new-book-about-our-nations-fear-of-flour.html.

"Sliced Bread Put Back on Sale; Housewives' Thumbs Safe Again." *New York Times*. March 9, 1943, 16. https://timesmachine.nytimes.com/timesmachine/1943/03/09/87411999.html?pageNumber=16.

SOURDOUGH

The British Museum (June 14, 2013). "How to make 2,000-year-old-bread" (Video). Youtube. Retrieved July 22, 2020.

TORTILLAS

Rodriguez, Cindy Y. "How a Mexican snack became an American staple." CNN. September 18, 2017. https://www.cnn.com/2015/01/21/living/feat-tortilla-chip-history-tailgating-eatocracy/index.html.

White City Shopping Ctr., LP v. PR Rests., LLC, 21 Mass. L. Rep. 565 (Mass. Super. Ct. 2006).

WHEAT

Hurshman, Rachel. "Brown Bread vs. Whole Wheat." *SF Gate*. December 12, 2018. https://healthyeating.sfgate.com/brown-bread-vs-whole-wheat-9104.html.

Chapter 4—Carnivorous Cravings: Things you didn't know about meat and seafood

BACON

Schultz, Colin. "The First Meal Eaten on the Moon Was Bacon." *Smithsonian.* April 8, 2014. https://www.smithsonianmag.com/smart -news/first-meal-eaten-moon-was-bacon.

Braun, Adee. "Turning Bacon into Bombs: The American Fat Salvage Committee." *The Atlantic.* April 18, 2014. https://www .theatlantic.com/health/archive/2014/04/reluctantly-turning -bacon-into-bombs-during-world-war-ii/360298/.

BARBECUE

"Longest barbecue marathon." *Guinness World Records.* https://www .guinnessworldrecords.com/world-records/longest-barbecue-marathon.

"Longest barbecue." *Guinness World Records.* https://www.guinness worldrecords.com/world-records/longest-barbecue.

BEEF

"Alpha-gal syndrome." Mayo Clinic. https://www.mayoclinic.org /diseases-conditions/alpha-gal-syndrome/symptoms-causes/syc -20428608.

CHICKEN

Mariani, John F. (1999). *The Encyclopedia of American Food and Drink.* New York: Lebhar-Friedman, pages 305–306.

Barton, Eric. "Why Japan celebrates Christmas with KFC." BBC. December 19, 2016. https://www.bbc.com/worklife/article/20161216 -why-japan-celebrates-christmas-with-kfc.

Martini, Frederic H., and Edwin F. Bartholomew. *Essentials of Anatomy and Physiology*. San Francisco: Benjamin Cummings Publishing Company, 2007, Page 201

Gorman, James. "It Could Be the Age of the Chicken, Geologically." *New York Times*. December 11, 2018. https://www.nytimes.com/2018 /12/11/science/chicken-anthropocene-archaeology.html.

EGGS

Fallaci, Oriana. "Alfred Hitchcock: Mr. Chastity." Sidney Gottlieb, ed. *Alfred Hitchcock: Interviews*. Univ. Press of Mississippi, 2003. 61.

Schwarcz, Joe. "You can determine the colour of an egg a chicken lays by looking at its earlobe." McGill University. April 18, 2019. https://www.mcgill.ca/oss/article/did-you-know-nutrition /you-can-determine-colour-egg-looking-chickens-earlobe.

GOAT

Palmer, Alex. "This Is Why Goats Randomly Faint." Best Life. November 9, 2018. https://bestlifeonline.com/this-is-why-goats -randomly-faint/.

HAMBURGER

"McDonald's 'wrong' to fire worker over cheese slice." January 26, 2010. BBC. http://news.bbc.co.uk/2/hi/europe/8481827.stm.

"BBQ mealworms and pigeon burgers on menu in UK." CBS News. https://www.cbsnews.com/pictures/bbq-mealworms-and -pigeon-burgers-on-menu-in-uk/.

HOT DOGS

Ewbank, Anne. "Why Michigan's Favorite Hot Dog Has a New York Name." Gastro Obscura. March 8, 2018. https://www.atlasobscura .com/articles/what-is-coney-dog-detroit.

"Longest hot dog." Guinness World Records. https://www.guinness worldrecords.com/world-records/longest-hot-dog.

"Taiwan Street Delights—Big Sausage Wrap Small Sausage." DanielFoodDiary.com. August 15, 2011. https://danielfooddiary .com/2011/08/15/taiwan-sausage/.

LAMB

"OECD-FAO Agricultural Outlook 2016–2025." Food and Agriculture Organization of the United Nations. Boulogne-Billancourt, France: OECD Publishing, 2016.

LOBSTER

"Made for the sea: Golf balls out of lobster shells." NBC News. March 31, 2011. http://www.nbcnews.com/id/42363588/ns/technology _and_science-innovation/t/made-sea-golf-balls-out-lobster -shells/.

"Lobster Ice Cream." Ben & Bill's Chocolate Emporium. http: //benandbills.net/ic_lobster.html.

Dembosky, April. "How the Lobster Clawed Its Way Up." *Mother Jones*. March/April 2006. https://www.motherjones.com/politics/2006/03/how-lobster-clawed-its-way/.

OYSTERS

Klein, Joanna. "Oysters, Despite What You've Heard, Are Always in Season." *New York Times*. May 5, 2017. https://www.nytimes.com/2017/05/05/science/oysters-summer-safe-r-months.html.

"King Coffin Bay Oyster." https://www.coffinbayoysterfarm.com.au/our-coffin-bay-oysters-range/king-oysters/.

PORK

"Prehistoric Predators: Hell Pig." *National Geographic*. http://natgeotv.com/ca/prehistoric-predators/videos.

Schwarcz, Joe. "Sweating like a pig." McGill Office for Science and Society. September 18, 2018. https://www.mcgill.ca/oss/article/health/sweating-pig.

Sifton, Sam. "A Field Guide to the American Sandwich." *New York Times*. April 14, 2015. https://www.nytimes.com/interactive/2015/04/14/dining/field-guide-to-the-sandwich.html?_r=0.

SALAMI

"Jewellery thefts that shocked the world." BBC. August 1, 2018. https://www.bbc.com/news/world-45036529.

SPAM

"Spam: The Meat They Loved to Hate." *Saturday Evening Post*. January 23, 2019. https://www.saturdayeveningpost.com/2019/01/spam-the -meat-they-loved-to-hate/.

SUSHI

Norwegian Institute for Water Research (NIVA). "Sea urchins: From pest to plate." ScienceDaily. August 9, 2017. www.sciencedaily .com/releases/2017/08/170809074010.htm.

Corson, Trevor. *The Story of Sushi: An Unlikely Saga of Raw Fish and Rice*. New York: Harper Perennial, 2008, page 143.

"Funazushi." Gastro Obscura. https://www.atlasobscura.com/foods /funazushi-fermented-fish-sushi.

TUNA

Ferdman, Roberto A. "How America fell out of love with canned tuna." *Washington Post*. August 18, 2014. https://www.washingtonpost .com/news/wonk/wp/2014/08/18/how-america-fell-out-of -love-with-canned-tuna/.

Chapter 6—Between-Meal Tidbits: Curious facts about snacks

ALMONDS

Hill, Mark Douglas. *The Aphrodisiac Encyclopaedia: A Compendium of Culinary Come-ons*. New York: Random House, 2012, page 42.

Do, Tiffany. "How the Government Is Reusing Almond Shells." Food Republic. March 19, 2018. https://www.foodrepublic.com /2018/03/19/reusing-almond-shells/.

Mucci, Kristy. "Green Almonds Are the Super-Seasonal Taste of Spring to Eat Right Now." *Saveur.* April 14, 2017.

CRACKERS

"Titanic survivor: world's most valuable biscuit up for auction." *The Guardian.* October 5, 2015. https://www.theguardian.com/uk -news/2015/oct/08/titanic-worlds-most-valuable-biscuit-up -for-auction.

Wolke, Robert L. "How the Cracker Got Those Holes." *South Florida Sun-Sentinel.* November 5, 1998. https://www.sun-sentinel.com/news /fl-xpm-1998-11-05-9811030448-story.html.

EGG ROLL

Koerth-Baker, Maggie. "What's the Difference?: Egg Roll vs. Spring Roll." *Mental Floss* May 24, 2016. https://www.mentalfloss .com/article/16080/whats-difference-egg-roll-vs-spring-roll.

FRENCH FRIES

"World's Longest Curly Fry: Arby's Customer Kim Medford Discovers 38-Inch Long Spud." Huffington Post. February 20, 2013. https://www.huffpost.com/entry/worlds-longest-curly-fry-arby.

GUM

Hendrickson, Robert. *The Great American Chewing Gum Book.* Chilton Book Company, 1976, page 143.

"San Luis Obispo's Bubblegum Alley." *Atlas Obscura.* https://www
.atlasobscura.com/places/bubblegum-alley.

Steinberg, Jim. "Susan Montgomery Williams, 47, had TV fame
from bubble-blowing." *Press-Telegram.* October 8, 2008. https://www
.presstelegram.com/2008/10/08/susan-montgomery-williams
-47-had-tv-fame-from-bubble-blowing/.

HUMMUS
"Lebanon claims latest title in 'Hummus War.'" CNN. May 9, 2010.
https://www.cnn.com/2010/WORLD/meast/05/09/lebanon
.hummus/index.html.

NACHOS
Haram, Karen. "The Legend of Nacho's Appetizer." *South Florida
Sun-Sentinel.* February 14, 2002. https://www.sun-sentinel.com
/news/fl-xpm-2002-02-14-0202120506-story.html.

Frank, Lee, and Rachel Anderson. *Ultimate Nachos: From Nachos and
Guacamole to Salsas and Cocktails.* New York: St. Martin's Griffin, 2013,
page 45.

PEANUT BUTTER
"Food Standard Innovations: Peanut Butter's Sticky Standard."
January 31, 2018. https://www.fda.gov/about-fda/histories-product
-regulation/food-standard-innovations-peanut-butters-sticky
-standard.

POPCORN

Petit, Charise. "Research unravels 'pop-ability' problem." *Purdue Exponent.* April 21, 2005. https://www.purdueexponent.org /campus/article_b811d3ce-5f79-5aad-8a45-a889002869a2 .html.

"Huehuetlahtolli." Miguel Leon-Portilla, and Earl Shorris, eds. *In the Language of Kings: An Anthology of Mesoamerican Literature.* New York: W.W. Norton & Company, 2002, page 266.

POTATO CHIPS

Davis, Rebecca, and Jake Heller. "Chips So Good You'll Have to Go to Jail to Get Them." NBC News. September 14, 2016. https://www.nbcnews.com/news/us-news/chips-so-good-you-ll -have-go-jail-get-them-n648241.

Lee, William E., et al. "Analysis of Food Crushing Sounds During Mastication: Total Sound Level Studies." *Journal of Texture Studies.* July 1990. https://onlinelibrary.wiley.com/doi/abs/10.1111/j.1745–4603 .1990.tb00473.x.

TORTILLA CHIPS

Torrisi, Lauren. "UK Restaurant Bakes Largest Tortilla Chip." ABC News. June 21, 2012. https://abcnews.go.com/blogs/lifestyle/2012 /06/uk-restaurant-bakes-largest-tortilla-chip/.

Collins, Glenn. "Pepsico Pushes a Star Performer. *New York Times.* November 3, 1994, section D, page 1.

YOGURT

Poutahidis, Theofilos, et al. "Probiotic microbes sustain youthful serum testosterone levels and testicular size in aging mice." *PLOS ONE* 9.1 (2014): e84877.

Chapter 7—Spice Up Your Life: Unexpected morsels about your favorite condiments, sauces, and spices

CINNAMON

Rodriguez et al., 2008 "New Cinnamon-Based Active Paper Packaging against Rhizopusstolonifer Food Spoilage." *Journal of Agricultural and Food Chemistry* 56.15 (2008): 6364. DOI: 10.1021/jf800699q.

Synan, Mariel. "Cinnamon's Spicy History." History.com. October 4, 2013. https://www.history.com/news/cinnamons-spicy-history.

HONEY

"Can you eat wasp honey?" pH7 science blog, University of Sheffield. September 17, 2015. https://www.ph7sheffield.com/post/2015/09/17/can-you-eat-wasp-honey.

https://clovermead.com/bee-beard/.

HOT SAUCE

Chile Pepper Institute. https://cpi.nmsu.edu/heat/.

Hertzberg, Richie. "Only Two Known Mammals Like Spicy Food." *National Geographic*. July 17, 2018. https://www.nationalgeographic.com/animals/2018/07/tree-shrews-pain-chili-peppers-news.

Cheslow, Daniella. "'Tabasco' Opera Makes Fiery Return In New Orleans." NPR. January 25, 2018. https://www.npr.org/sections/thetwo-way/2018/01/25/580713942/tabasco-opera-makes-fiery-return-in-new-orleans.

KETCHUP

Brownlee, John. "How 500 Years of Weird Condiment History Designed the Heinz Ketchup Bottle." *Fast Company*. December 21, 2013. https://www.fastcompany.com/1673352/how-500-years-of-weird-condiment-history-designed-the-heinz-ketchup-bottle.

Rawsthorn, Alice. "An Icon, Despite Itself." *New York Times*. April 12, 2009. https://www.nytimes.com/2009/04/13/fashion/13iht-design13.html?_r=1.

Braun, Adee. "The Tomato Pill Craze." Gastro Obscura. October 16, 2017. https://www.atlasobscura.com/articles/tomato-pill.

MAYONNAISE

Dean, Sam. "On the Etymology of the Word Mayonnaise." *Bon Appetit*. April 4, 2013. https://www.bonappetit.com/test-kitchen/ingredients/article/on-the-etymology-of-the-word-mayonnaise.

Torborg, Liz. "Mayo Clinic Q and A: Getting rid of head lice." Mayo Clinic. JUly 29, 2017. https://newsnetwork.mayoclinic.org/discussion/mayo-clinic-q-and-a-getting-rid-of-head-lice/.

Whitten, Sarah. "Mayonnaise debunks refrigerator myth and wins a seat at the table." CNBC. June 28, 2016. https://www.cnbc.com/2016/06/28/mayonnaise-debunks-refridgerator-myth-and-wins-a-seat-at-the-table-.html.

MUSTARD

"Where does Canada lead the world in crop production globally? (The answer might surprise you!)" Canada West Foundation. December 21, 2017. https://cwf.ca/research/publications/where-does-canada-lead-the-world-in-crop-production-globally-the-answer-might-surprise-you/.

https://mustardmuseum.com/.

SALAD DRESSING

Fischer, Lisa. "The story of the Nebraska cowboy who invented ranch dressing." *World-Herald News Service*. February 13, 2014. https://omaha.com/entertainment/the-story-of-the-nebraska-cowboy-who-invented-ranch-dressing/article_8f2d023e-5cf7-521f-aeda-55c59729583f.html.

Blaskovich, Sarah. "Dallas pizza shop gets $2,000 donation — all from a 'master-level troll' over ranch dressing." *Dallas Morning News*. March 20, 2020. https://www.dallasnews.com/food/restaurant-news/2020/03/20/hidden-valley-ranch-donates-2000-to-cane-rosso-pizza-dallas-during-coronavirus-struggle/.

SALSA

Vann, Mick. "Who's a Pepper?" *Austin Chronicle.* August 22, 2008. https://www.austinchronicle.com/food/2008-08-22/663211/.

Portal, Leslie. "Mindful of Ketchup Flap, USDA Rules Salsa Is a School Vegetable." *Chicago Tribune.* July 1, 1998. https://www.chicagotribune.com/news/ct-xpm-1998-07-01-9807010037-story.html.

"Pico de Gallo." Epicurious. https://www.epicurious.com/recipes/food/views/pico-de-gallo-358971.

SOY SAUCE

Daniels, Stephen. "Antioxidant-rich soy sauce could protect against CVD." nutraingredients.com. June 6, 2006. https://www.nutraingredients.com/Article/2006/06/06/Antioxidant-rich-soy-sauce-could-protect-against-CVD.

Chapter 8—Strange Sips: Odd bits about beverages and libations

BEER

Smith, Oliver. "The surprising countries that consume the most beer per capita." *The Telegraph.* August 3, 2018. https://www.telegraph.co.uk/travel/maps-and-graphics/beer-consumption-per-capita-countries/.

"The U.S Beer Industry 2019." https://www.nbwa.org/resources/industry-fast-facts.

Mack, Zach. "The Differences Between Lager and Ale, Explained." Thrillist. April 21, 2020. https://www.thrillist.com/drink/nation /difference-between-lager-vs-ale.

Smith, K. Annabelle. "When Heineken Bottles Were Square." *Smithsonian*. May 15, 2013. https://www.smithsonianmag.com/arts -culture/when-heineken-bottles-were-square-62138490/.

Jackson, Michael. "Indulge in the Bavarian Weiss." Beer Hunter. September 2, 1998. http://www.beerhunter.com/documents/19133 —000058.html.

Knapp, Alex. "For Winning the Nobel Prize, Niels Bohr Got a House with Free Beer." *Forbes*. November 28, 2012. https://www .forbes.com/sites/alexknapp/2012/11/28/for-winning-the-nobel -prize-niels-bohr-got-a-house-with-free-beer/#64e3b89b2759.

COFFEE

"Origin and History of Instant Coffee." Accessed July 12, 2020. http://www.historyofcoffee.net/coffee-history/instant-coffee -history.

Smith, Oliver. "Mapped: The countries that drink the most coffee." *The Telegraph*. October 1, 2017. https://www.telegraph.co.uk/travel /maps-and-graphics/countries-that-drink-the-most-coffee/.

Martinez, Victoria. "Once upon a time, when coffee was illegal in Sweden . . . say what now?" The Local SE. July 2, 2018. https://www.thelocal.se/20180702/why-coffee-was-banned-in -sweden-five-times.

Carder, Gemma, et al. "The animal welfare implications of civet coffee tourism in Bali." *Animal Welfare* 25.2 (2016): 199–205.

"Caffeine content for coffee, tea, soda and more." Mayo Clinic. https://www.mayoclinic.org/healthy-lifestyle/nutrition-and-healthy -eating/in-depth/caffeine/art-20049372.

Maia, L., and A. De Mendonça. "Does caffeine intake protect from Alzheimer's disease?" *European Journal of Neurology* 9.4 (2002): 377–382.

EGGNOG

Klein, Christopher. "When Eggnog Sparked a Riot at West Point." History.com. August 22, 2018. https://www.history.com/news /when-eggnog-sparked-a-riot-at-west-point.

HOT CHOCOLATE

"Hot Chocolate History." The Nibble. December 2006. http://www .thenibble.com/reviews/main/beverages/cocoas/hot-chocolate -overview2.asp.

Cocking, Lauren. "The Rambunctious, Elitist Chocolate Houses of 18th-Century London." Gastro Obscura. November 28, 2018. https: //www.atlasobscura.com/articles/history-of-gentlemens-clubs.

Synan, Mariel. "Hot Chocolate for Strength." History.com. November 8, 2013. https://www.history.com/news/hot-chocolate -for-strength.

"Hot Cocoa Tops Red Wine And Tea In Antioxidants; May Be Healthier Choice." November 6, 2003. Science Daily. https://www.sciencedaily.com/releases/2003/11/031106051159.htm.

LEMONADE

Palmer, Brian. "Why Do We Drink Lemonade When It's Hot Out?" *Slate*. July 17, 2013. https://slate.com/technology/2013/07/lemonade-on-a-hot-day-why-are-acidic-drinks-refreshing.html.

Bertsche, Rachel. "Police Shut Down Girls' Lemonade Stand for Ridiculous Reason." Yahoo Parentings. June 10, 2015. https://www.yahoo.com/news/police-shut-down-girls-lemonade-stand-for-121207241667.html.

Campisi, Jessica and Saeed Ahmed. "For kids getting busted for running lemonade stands without permits, these guys are here to help." CNN. June 11, 2018. https://www.cnn.com/2018/06/11/us/lemonade-stands-country-time-trnd/index.html.

Chetwynd, Josh. *How the Hot Dog Found Its Bun: Accidental Discoveries and Unexpected Inspirations That Shape What We Eat and Drink.* Rowman & Littlefield, 2012, page 117.

MILK

Lite, Jordan. "Cows with names make more milk." *Scientific American*. January 28, 2009. https://blogs.scientificamerican.com/news-blog/cows-with-names-make-more-milk-2009-01-28/.

Holmberg, Sara, and Anders Thelin. "High dairy fat intake related to less central obesity: a male cohort study with 12 years' follow-up." *Scandinavian Journal of Primary Health Care* 31.2 (2013): 89–94.

Samgina, T. Yu, et al. "Composition and antimicrobial activity of the skin peptidome of Russian brown frog Rana temporaria." *Journal of Proteome Research* 11.12 (2012): 6213–6222.

O'Connell, Rebecca. "10 Non-Cow Milk Products You Can Try." *Mental Floss.* January 5, 2016. https://www.mentalfloss.com/article /73217/10-non-cow-milk-products-you-can-try.

SODA

Smith, Andrew, and Bruce Kraig, eds. *The Oxford Encyclopedia of Food and Drink in America.* Vol. 1. Oxford University Press, 2013, page 805.

Jorgensen, Janice. *Encyclopedia of Consumer Brands.* St. James Press, 1994, page 168.

"A Morning Cola Instead of Coffee?" *New York Times.* January 20, 1988.

"Fanta and the Nazis." Snopes.com. September 13, 2004. https: //www.snopes.com/fact-check/the-reich-stuff/

SPIRITS

Sachs, Tony. "The Rum the British Navy Once Rationed to Sailors Is Now Highly Coveted—and Surprisingly Good." *Robb Report.* July 31, 2020. https://robbreport.com/food-drink/spirits /black-tot-rum-british-navy-ration-for-sale-2939203/.

Sample, Ian. "Tequila turned into diamonds." *The Guardian*. November 12, 2008. https://www.theguardian.com/science/2008/nov/13/agriculture-mexico-tequila-diamonds.

TEA

Ferdman, Roberto. "Where the world's biggest tea drinkers are." *Quartz*. https://qz.com/168690/where-the-worlds-biggest-tea-drinkers-are/.

Begley, Sarah. "A Brief History of the Tea Bag." *TIME*. September 3, 2015. https://time.com/3996712/a-brief-history-of-the-tea-bag.

Hollins, Seren Charrington. *A Dark History of Tea*. Havertown, PA: Pen & Sword Books Limited, 2020, page 74.

"Family Food 2015." Department for Environment, Food & Rural Affairs. 2017. https://assets.publishing.service.gov.uk/government/uploads/system/uploads/attachment_data/file/597667/Family_Food_2015-09mar17.pdf.

"Sect where blessings pour from a teapot." *Sydney Morning Herald*. March 4, 2005. https://www.religionnewsblog.com/10448/sect-where-blessings-pour-from-a-teapot.

"The Year Britain Bought Up All the Tea in the World." *Teabox*. June 22, 2016. https://blog.teabox.com/year-britain-bought-tea-world.

WINE

"The Roman Wine of Speyer: The Oldest Wine of the World That's Still Liquid." Deutsches Weininstitut. https://web.archive

.org/web/20140426215229/http://www.deutscheweine.de/icc/Internet-EN/nav/4b4/4b470693-6826-7e21-e66b-48554c41ed8b%26_ic_uCon%3D016407a8-5735-f431-aecd-f9916f135e25.

St. Fleur, Nicholas. "Wine From Prehistoric Georgia with an 8,000-Year-Old Vintage." *New York Times*. November 13, 2017. https://www.nytimes.com/2017/11/13/science/georgia-oldest-wine.html.

Wiseman, Ed. "Did Prince Charles really modify his Aston Martin to run on wine—and should we do the same?" *Telegraph*. November 8, 2018. https://www.telegraph.co.uk/cars/features/did-prince-charles-really-modify-aston-martin-run-wine-should/.

North, Adrian C., David J. Hargreaves, and Jennifer McKendrick. "The influence of in-store music on wine selections." *Journal of Applied Psychology* 84.2 (1999): 271.

Gao, Sally. "A Brief Introduction to Snake Wine." The Culture Trip. January 13, 2017. https://theculturetrip.com/asia/hong-kong/articles/a-brief-introduction-to-snake-wine/.

Scattergood, Amy. "Saved From Prohibition by Holy Wine." *Smithsonian*. June 2012. https://www.smithsonianmag.com/travel/saved-from-prohibition-by-holy-wine-88250788/.

Plato. *Plato Laws 1 & 2*. Translated by Susan Sauve Meyer. London: Oxford University Press, 2015, page 64.

Chapter 9—Sweet Endings: Peculiar origins and info about beloved desserts

CAKE

Fraser, Antonia. *Marie Antoinette: The Journey.* New York: Anchor, 2002, page 135.

"Celebrating Not-So-German Chocolate Cake." NPR. June 23, 2007. https://www.npr.org/templates/story/story.php?storyId =11331541.

Panati, Charles. *Extraordinary Origins of Everyday Things.* New York: Harper & Row, 1987, page 32.

CANDY

Christen, Arden G., and Joan A. Christen. "William J. Morrison (1860–1926). Co-inventor of the cotton candy machine." *Journal of the History of Dentistry* 53.2 (2005): 51–56.

"The History of PEZ." https://us.pez.com/pages/history.

Fawcett, Kristin. "The Most Popular Halloween Candy in Each State." *Mental Floss.* September 24, 2018. https://www.mentalfloss .com/article/505083/united-states-sweetness-most-popular -halloween-candy-across-us.

"Tootsie Gallery: How Many Licks Does It Take?" Tootsie Roll Industries. https://tootsie.com/howmanylick-experiments.

CANDY BARS

Mikkelson, David. "Baby Ruth." Snopes.com. https://www.snopes.com/fact-check/baby-ruth/.

"World's weirdest Kit Kat candy bars." CBS News. September 19, 2011. https://www.cbsnews.com/pictures/worlds-weirdest-kit-kat-candy-bars/.

"Butterfinger Buzz (Caffeinated)." Candyblog. February 9, 2009. http://www.candyblog.net/blog/item/butterfinger_buzz.

"Largest chocolate bar by area." Guinness World Records. https://www.guinnessworldrecords.com/world-records/longest-chocolate-bar.

CARAMEL

"Lancaster Caramel Company." *Hershey Community Archives*. September 6, 2018. https://hersheyarchives.org/encyclopedia/lancaster-caramel-company/.

"The Accidental Origin of Caramel Apples." Rocky Mountain Chocolate Factory. https://trending.rmcf.com/chocolate-facts/accidental-origin-caramel-apples.

CHOCOLATE

"The Fortress Stilt Fisherman Indulgence." https://www.fortressresortandspa.com/dining/the-fortress-stilt-fisherman-indulgence.html.

Janik, Rachel. "How the Hershey's Kiss Conquered Valentine's Day." *TIME*. February 14, 2015. https://time.com/3707086/hershey-kiss-history-valentines/.

Jensen, K. Thor. "The Scandalous Story Behind M&Ms' Name." OMG Facts. http://omgfacts.com/the-scandalous-story-behind-mms-name/.

COOKIES

Scribner, Herb. "Nabisco uncaged its animal crackers after 116 years. Here's why." *Deseret News*. August 21, 2018. https://www.deseret.com/2018/8/21/20651711/nabisco-uncaged-its-animal-crackers-after-116-years-here-s-why.

Jones, Brian Jay. *Jim Henson: The Biography*. New York: Ballantine Books, 2015, page 136.

ÉCLAIR

"Éclair—Why Is It Named After Lightning?" Lexicolatry. May 27, 2015. http://www.lexicolatry.com/2015/05/eclair-why-is-it-named-after-lightning.html.

DOUGHNUTS

Panati, Charles. *Extraordinary Origins of Everyday Things*. New York: Harper & Row, 1987, page 415.

FORTUNE COOKIES

Lee, Jennifer 8. "Who Needs Giacomo? Bet on the Fortune Cookie." *New York Times*. May 11, 2005. https://www.nytimes.com/2005/05/11/nyregion/who-needs-giacomo-bet-on-the-fortune-cookie.html.

Lee, Jennifer 8. "The fortune cookie's origin: Solving a riddle wrapped in a mystery inside a cookie." *New York Times.* January 6, 2008. https://www.nytimes.com/2008/01/16/travel/16iht-fortune .9260526.html?login=smartlock&auth=login-smartlock.

ICE CREAM

Dreifus, Claudia. "Passing the Scoop: Ben & Jerry." *New York Times Magazine.* December 18, 1994. Section 6, Page 38.

Hatcher, Cindy. "The Man with The Million-Dollar Taste Buds." August 6, 2002. https://www.cookinglight.com/cooking-101/meet -the-chef/the-man-with-the-million-dollar-taste-buds.

National Research Council. *Lost Crops of the Incas: Little-Known Plants of the Andes with Promise for Worldwide Cultivation.* National Academies Press, 1989, pages 276–285.

Harris, Jenn. "Glow-in-the-dark jellyfish ice cream—for $225, you can have a scoop." *Los Angeles Times.* November 6, 2013. https: //www.latimes.com/food/dailydish/la-dd-jellyfish-ice-cream -20131106-story.html.

MARSHMALLOWS

Goldstein, Darra. *The Oxford Companion to Sugar and Sweets.* Oxford University Press, 2015, page 430.

MILKSHAKES

Boadle, Anthony. "Closest CIA bid to kill Castro was poisoned drink." Reuters. July 5, 2007. https://www.reuters.com/article/us-cuba

-cia/closest-cia-bid-to-kill-castro-was-poisoned-drink
-idUSN0427935120070705.

"Coffee Cabinet." Gastro Obscura. https://www.atlasobscura.com
/foods/coffee-cabinet-rhode-island.

PIE

"Toy company Wham-O produces first Frisbees." History.com.
November 24, 2009. https://www.history.com/this-day-in-history
/toy-company-wham-o-produces-first-frisbees.

TIRAMISU

Pearlman, Robert Z. "Italian Takeout: Italy's 1st Spacewalking
Astronaut Shares Tiramisu in Space." Space.com. July 9, 2013.
https://www.space.com/21891-italian-astroanut-spacewalk
-space-food.html.

TWINKIES

Belcher, Jerry. "Man Who Concocted the Twinkie Dies: James A.
Dewar's Treat Is Part of America's Diet and Folklore." *Los Angeles
Times*. July 3, 1985. https://www.latimes.com/archives/la-xpm-1985
-07-03-me-10272-story.html.

WEDDING CAKE

Kraig, Bruce. *The Oxford Encyclopedia of Food and Drink in America*, Volume
1. 2013. Page 567.